The *Shiva-Suṭra-Vimarṣinī* of Kṣēmarāja

Sri Garib Das Oriental Series No.174

The
Shiva-Sutra-Vimarṣinī
of Kṣēmarāja

Translated Into English
By
P.T. Shrinivas Iyengar
Principal, Mrs. A.V.N. College, Vishakhapatnam

Sri Satguru Publications
A Division of
Indian Books Centre
Delhi - India

Published by
Sri Satguru Publications,
Indological and Oriental Publishers
A Division of
Indian Books Centre
40/5, Shakti Nagar,
Delhi-110007
India

Email: ibcindia@vsnl.com
Website: http://www.indianbookscentre.com

First Edition; Allahabad, 1912
Second Edition ; Delhi, 1994
Reprinted ; 2007

ISBN 81-7030-390-7

Printed at Chawla Offset Printers, Delhi 110 052

Contents

Introduction vii

Preliminary Note xix

Unmēṣa-I SHĀMBHAVOPĀYA 1

Unmēṣa-II SHĀKṬOPĀYA 23

Unmēṣa-III ĀNĀVOPĀYA 36

Notes 69

Indices 81

Introduction

The Pāñcharātra and the Pāshupata, the Jaina and The Bauddha, all these systems, arose in India after the supremacy of the Veda and the Vedānta was successfully challenged by the Sāṅkhya. All these schools of thought were elaborated by members of ascetic orders, open to men of low caste and to women, and following rules more or less opposed to those of the orthodox fourth āshrama of the Shāstra (*varṇāshramakṛitairdharmair-viparītam kvachit samam*, Mahābhār. xii. 284). All the non-Vedic systems started from the philosophical analysis of experience arrived at by the Sāṅkhya into twenty-five tattvas and extended it. The Yoga supplemented it by predicating an Īshvarā. This Īshvarā of Yoga is a colourless person, possessing none of the well-known characteristics of the Godhead, a special puruṣa untouched by evil, his only function being that of a Teacher (*Yog. Sū.*, i, 24-6); An early form of the Pāñcharātra doctrine attributed to Nārada and called the Sāttvata Dharma, definitely recognized Viṣṇu as the twenty-sixth principle, beyond the twenty-five recognized by the Sāṅkhya. The Lord and the individual are in this system related as *buddha* and the *budhyamāna*, the all-knowing and the little-knowing, the all and the fraction. (*Ib.* 308, 309, 319). This early compromise between the Sāṅkhya and the Vedānta represents also the Spirit of the fundamental teaching of the Bhagavadgītā.

Another early form of the Pāñcharātra cult was that of Pañchashika, as described in the *Mahābhārata* (xii. 320). This shows a further development of the Sāṅkhya categories. The Elements of the Universe are here thirty Kalās or Guṇas—words having a specific, technical sense in other schools. Sulabhā expounds Pañchashika's system to Janaka, King of Mithilā and describes the thirty categories as (1-10) the ten Indriyas, (11) Manas, (12) Buddhi, (13) Sattva, (14) Ahaṁkāra, (15) Pṛithakkalā Samūhasya Sāmagryam (the disposition of the different kalās while in union), (16) Saṅghāta, a complex wherein inhere (17) Prakṛiti, (18) Vyakti, unmanifest and manifest matter, (19) the union of the correlates (dvandva-yoga), pleasure and pain, old age and death, gain and loss, love and hate, (20) Kāla, (21-25) the five gross elements, (26-27) the relation and union of Sat and Asat (Sadasadbhāvayogau), (28) Vidhi, (29) Shukra, and (30) bala. All creatures are born from a union of these kalās. Prof. Hopkins has pointed out that the *Bhagavad-gītā,* which belongs also to the Pāñcharātra School, also called the School of the Bhāgavatas, enumerates a set of 31 forms of the Kṣētram, 31 modifications of matter, *i.e.,* 5 gross elements, Ahaṁkāra, Buddhi, Avyaktam (corresponding to Prakṛiti), 11 indriyas (including manas), 5 objects of sense, love, hate, pleasure, pain, saṅghāta, chētanā and dhṛiti (xii. 5-6). Above these are the four forms of Paramātmā, identified in these Schools with Viṣṇu or Nārāyaṇa, *i.e.* Vāsudēva, Saṅkarṣaṇa, Pradyumna and Aniruddha.

Asita Dēvala propounds to Nārada, a slightly similar analysis of the universe (Mahābhār. xii-275). The five gross Elements and Time make up six rāshis. When bhāva and abhāva are added to them, they become the eight bhūtas. The sense-organs, the sense-objects, the sense-functions are five-fold. Chitta is superior to the Saṅghāta, complex, of the sense-organs; manas is superior to Chitta, and Buddhi to manas. These are eight Jñānēndriyas. There are five organs of action, and with bala, they are six. There are three bhāvas, Sāttvika, Tāmasa and Rājasa. These fourteen organs and three bhāvas make up the seventeen guṇas. The dēhī, eternal, embodied being is the eighteenth. These eighteen, the body and bodily heat make up the Saṅghāta of twenty. Asīta Dēvala, in another place, is said to be a devotee of Shiva; so the above analysis is probably one of the early speculations of the Shaiva schools.

In the course of ages, the Shaivas worked out a definite scheme of tattvas, divided into three classes, *(i)* the Ātma-tattva consisting of 32 principles, *viz.* the twenty-five Sāṅkhya tattvas, guṇa, the five-fold envelope of the Puruṣa, *i.e.* (i) Niyati (the force of Karma), (2) Kāla (Time), (3) Rāga (latent desire), (4) Vidyā (which links Ātmā to Buddhi), and (5) Kālā, (differentiated consciousness), and Māyā, the root of all these, (ii) three Vidyātattvas, Shuddhavidyā, Īshvara and Sadāshiva, and (iii) the Shivatattva being the highest. It would be an interesting study to compare this final Shaiva scheme of tattvas with the tentative ones that preceded it; but it cannot be undertaken here.

Besides the philosophy of the Sāṅkhya, these non-vedic schools absorbed the disciplines of the Yoga. The Pāñcharātra School selected one Yoga discipline—Īshvara-Praṇidhāna, Service of the Lord (Yoga. Sūt., 23), as its chief characteristic. The Bhagavad-Gītā, the scripture *par excellence,* of this school, uses the word Yoga mostly in the sense of devotion to Kṛiṣṇa—Vāsudēva. Its final declaration—"give up all dharma (the rules prescribed in all schools), take refuge in me alone, I will release you from all sin; do not grieve,"—has for more than two thousand years been the basic teaching of the followers of Viṣṇu. The Shaiva cults have attached more importance to other forms of the Yoga discipline, *e.g.,* meditation, the eight-limbed Yoga, and the recitation of mantras; so much so that the

Shiva-Sūtra here translated is practically but a manual of Yoga. With the analysis of the universe taught by the Sāṅkhya and the disciplines of the Yoga, were welded in these Vaiṣṇava and Shaiva Schools, also the love of a personal God and the belief that God's grace is a necessary antecedent of individual Salvation. This provision for devotion to a distinct personal God enabled these cults to oust their rivals, the Bauddha and the Jaina, and to continue to our days to be the living religions of India, in spite of the supposed superiority of the Vedānta.

The Shaiva cult broke up in the course of time into three schools. The first is the South Indian School, which calls itself the Shaiva Siddhanta. Its canon consists of 28 Āgamas, only one of which, *Shrīchandrajñāna,* is quoted in this work. There are besides numerous Tamil works, regarded as authoritative by the South Indian Shaivas. The second is the Gujarat School, called Lakulīsha Pāshupatam,[1] described by the author of the *Sarvadarshanasaṅgraha;* but not one of their works has yet been discovered. The third is the Kāshmiri School.

Buhler in his *Detailed Report of a Tour in Search of Sanskrit Mss* (1877), falls into two serious errors in his account of this school. He divides it "into two classes, according to the two great Shaiva Schools of Kashmir: (*a*) works referring to the so-called Spanda Shāstra of Vasugupta, (*b*) works belonging to the Pratyabhijñā Shāstra of Somānanda and Utpala." As a matter of fact, the Kāshmiri School is not two-fold; it is true that like every other school it received some slight accretions when it passed down the stream of tradition, but the doctrinal differences even between Vasugupta, its founder, and Kṣēmarājā, one of its latest teachers, are not sufficiently pronounced to justify their being regarded as belonging to two different schools. Spanda is the goal and Pratyabhijñā, the means of reaching it, and the Spanda Shāstram and the Pratyabhijñā Shāstram are identical. Buhler identifies the Shaivadarshana described in the VII chapter of *Sarvadarshanasaṅgraha* with Vasugupta's system. This is wrong. The Shaivadarshana of Sāyana-Mādhava is the South Indian School, called the 'Shaiva Siddhānta' and based on the 28 Shaiva Āgamas. In his account Sāyana Mādhava frequently quotes from the *Mṛigendra Āgama,* which is the jñānapāda of the *Kāmika,* the first of the South Indian Āgamas, and also the *Pauṣkara, Karaṇa, Kiraṇa,* and other Āgamas of the same series, and does not at all refer to any books or authors of Kāshmir.

This Kāshmiri Shaiva School was founded by Vasugupta who, according to the commentary on the first Sūtra of this work, "discovered" a set of Shiva-Sūtras engraved on stone and taught the doctrines therein contained to his disciple, Kallata. Buhler has determined the dates of the chief teachers of the Kāshmiri School and given a list of most of their works, Mss. of which he purchased in Kāshmir.

The best known teachers are:

1. Vasugupta, latter half of the VIII century. "Discovered" *Shiva-Sūtras.* Wrote *Spandakārikā, Siddhāntachandrika, Stotrāvalī.* Vasugupta's *Spandakārikā* also called *Spandasūtra* attributed by Utpala and Bhāskara to Kallata.

2. Kallata, Vasugupta's disciple, contemporary of Avanti-varman, King of Kāshmir (855-884 A.D.), wrote *Spandasarvasva,* a commentary on Vasugupta's *Spandakārikā.*

3. Pradyumna, cousin and disciple of Kallata.

4. Prajñārjuna, disciple of Pradyumna.

5. Mahādēva, disciple of Prajñārjuna.

6. Somānanda-nātha, wrote *Shivadṛishti* referred to by Sāyana-Mādhva.

7. Utpala, disciple of the above, (*cir.* 930-950 A.D. wrote *Spandapradīpikā*, a commentary on *Spandakārikā*), *Ajadapramātrisiddhi*, *Parameshvarastotrāvalī*, *Īshvarapratyabhijñā Sūtra*.

8. Nārāyana, contemporary of Utpala, wrote *Stavachintāmaṇi*, *Sādhanadīpikā*.

9. Rāmakantha, pupil of Utpala, wrote *Spandavivaraṇasaramātra*, being the tippana on Kallata's *Spandasarvasva*, itself a tīkā of *Spandakārikā*.

10. Shrī Kantha, son and disciple of Mahādeva.

11. Lakshmaṇagupta, disciple of Utpala (*cir.* 950-975 A.D.).

12. Bhāskara, disciple of Shrī Kantha, wrote a Vārtika on Shiva-Sūtra, of which Buhler secured an incomplete copy.

13. Abhinava Gupta (*cir.* 993-1085 A.D.), prashiṣya of Utpala and of Nārāyaṇa, disciple of Lakṣmaṇa Gupta, wrote numerous works on various subjects; including a *Bhagavad Gītā Tīkā;* his known works on Spanda-Shāstra being *Īshvarapratyabhijñā-Sūtra-vṛitti (bṛihatī* and *laghu)*, *Tantrasāra*, *Tantrāloka*, *Bimbapratibimbavāda;* *Parmārthasaṅgraha*, *Bodhapañchadashikā*, *Bhairavārādhana*, *Parātrimshikā*, *Bhairavaṣtava* (for a list of his other works, *Vide* Preface to *Dhvanyāloka*, by the late Pundit Durgā Prasād).

14. *Kṣemarājā*, pupil of Abhinavagupta, sometimes called Kṣemendra, but to be carefully distinguished from Kṣēmēndra, another pupil of Abhinava. This latter was a Vaiṣṇava and wrote numerous works, among others, a condensed translation of *Bṛihatkathā* of Guṇādhya, condensation of *Bhārata* and *Rāmāyaṇa*, *Kalāvilāsa*, *Samayamātṛikā*. Kṣēmaṛājā wrote

Pratyabhijñāhṛidaya, *Smbapañhchāshikāvivaraṇa*, *Spandanirṇaya*, being a commentary on the *Spandakārikā* *Spandasandoha*, *Svachchandodyota*, commentaries on Ūtpala's *Parameshastotrāvali*, Nārāyaṇa's *Stavachintāmaṇi*, Abhinava's *Paramarthasaṅgraha*. But Buhler seems not to have come across Kṣēmarājā's most important work, *Shivā-sūtra-vimarshinī* which he does not even mention. He obtained two copies of the text of the *Shiva-sūtra*, which he calls *Spanda-sūtra*, as also an incomplete copy of a Vārtika on the same by Bhāskara, already referred to.

My attention was drawn to the Shiva-sūtras from their being quoted by Bhāskararāya, a writer of the XVIII century in his Lalitāsahasranāmabhāṣya. Bhāskararāya quotes also Kṣēmarājā, and more frequently, Kriṣṇadāsa's *Vārtika*, a versified form of Kṣēmarajā's *Vimarshinī*. I got a copy of the *Shiva-sūtra-Vimarshinī* from Mr. Govinda Das of Benares, and from his copy I have made this translation, with the help of Mr. Bhattanātha Svāmi, Sanskrit Lecturer, Mrs. A.V.N. College, Vizagapatam.

The *Shiva-sūtra* is, as I have already remarked, a Manual of Yoga. It is divided into three Unmēṣas, each treating of one particular means, Upāya, for reaching independence, Svachchhanda. The first is the Shāmbhavopāya, the specific Shaiva discipline and corresponds to the Jñānamārga of the Vedāntis, and what is called in the Bhagavad-Gītā, the jñānayoga of the Sāṅkhyas (iii, 3), also the avyaktā gatiḥ (xii, 5). The second, the Shāktopāya is the same as Shākta discipline and consists in the use of mantras and attainment of knowledge by their means. The third called the Āṇavopāya is the aṣtāṅga yoga of Patañjali. The three Upāyas are treated in the order of their worth; the Shāmbhava being the first and most excellent, and the Āṇava being the least worthy and not recognized by Vasugupta in his *Spandakārikā*.

The aim of the Shāmbhavopāya is to get rid of the three malas, impurities, that obstruct the light of consciousness, chaitanyam, that is the ātmā. These impurities are three, the first is the āṇava mala, the defect due to man, who in reality is identical with Shiva, falsely deeming himself to be a limited being, devoid of independence. This āṇava mala is called in this work the bondage of (limited) jñāna. The next is the Māyā mala, the root of the manifested universe, extending from the tattva Kalā that unites Ātmā to Buddhi and thus begets ordinary consciousness down to the gross element, earth. This is called in this work, Yonivarga. The third mala is Karma, called in this Shiva-sūtra, Kalāsharīram, the deposits of pleasure and pain. All these malas are directed by Shuddha Māyā, otherwise Shivashakti or Bindu, called here Mātṛikā. She is the creatrix of the world, and the letters A to Kṣa form her body. She is the Kuṇḍalinī, wound round the heart of the Pashu, the man who is under the power of Shuddha Māyā. She, assisted by troops of subordinate shaktis, seated in various pīthas, stations, in the rope of Brahmā, from the Mūlādhāra to the Brahmarandhra, urges men constantly to the experience of the objective universe. If there is an interval between two successive states of consciousness, the pure light of the Ātmā will shine through; but the Shaktis so urge man from experience to experience that such an interval cannot be attained. By the practice of introspective meditation, it is possible to sense momentary intervals between two consecutive states of consciousness, when the supreme light flashes forth and the man becomes a Bhairava, is conscious of himself as the universal, unconditioned consciousness, that is Shiva. This state is the Shāmbhava, which gives its name to this Upāya. If this pure light of consciousness is turned on the Shaktichakra, man will conquer the limitations forged for him by Shuddha Māyā. The bliss of the fourth state Turyābhoga, will constantly illuminate his experience of the usual three, jāgrat, svapna and Paśupati. Such a man is no more Pashu but a Virēsha. He is master of Ichchhā shakti, his mere desire is Umā, and the visible world is his body.

Another form of the Shāmbhavopāya is meditation on the highest Shiva Tattva, called in this work, Shuddha Tattva. By meditation on the Universe as being filled with Paramashiva, one rises to the rank of Sadāshiva, the Lord of the Manifested Universe. For attaining this, one should constantly dwell on the thought, "I am the ātmā of the universe, Shiva." To him the distinction between subject and object disappears and he reaches the bliss of Samādhi. Then by meditation on the shakti chakra he gets lordship over the chakras and the miraculous powers, siddhis, open to yogīs; and he obtains the highest siddhi of all mantravīrya, *i.e.*, power to discern and use of efficacy of mantras.

The Second Unmēṣa deals with the Shāktopāya and this is therefore a Mantrashāstra. A Mantra is a mere concatenation of sounds, absolutely inefficacious till the chitta attains unity with the divinity behind the Mantra. Effort is the only means to bring about this union. The Mantras are the body of Shakti, the Mātṛikā. She is latent in the ordinary man, like a sleeping serpent coiled round the spark of light concealed in the heart. The concentration of this spark on her, rouses her; the coiled one becomes straight, and when she is mastered, the man attains Māntravīrya. Long before he attains Mantravīrya, he feels an increase of intellectual power and a limited bliss. This is mita siddhi, ordinary acquisition, but when true knowledge rises, he reaches the state called Khēcharī, the state of Shiva. But the knowledge of Mantras, correspondences between letters and their shaktis, which constitutes the Mātṛikā Chakra, has to be learned from a Guru. The main principles of the Mātṛikā Chakra are these: The vowels indicate the shaktis, *a,* the jñāna shakti, *i,* the ichchhā shakti and *u* the kriyā shakti. The consonants indicate the objective universe. The 25 letters from *ka* to *ma* represent the lower 25 tattvas; of the Shiva school. The other letters represent the higher tattvas; and *kṣa* the last is the prāṇa-bīja, the life-seed. A man who has acquired a knowledge of the Mātṛikā Chakra, must try to transcend the limitations of his body; if not, he will become a prey to illusions.

The third Unmeṣa deals with the Aṇavopāya. The Puruṣa who identifies the Ātmā with the chitta is the Aṇu, enclosed in three veils. The first veil is the gross body, the next one is the eight-fold puri, the subtle body, composed of Prakṛiti, Guṇas, Buddhi, Ahaṅkāra, manas, organs, subtle elements (tanmātras) and gross elements (bhūtas), which form a saṅghāta of twenty. The third is the causal envelope, Kañchuka, composed of Niyati, Kāla, Rāga, Vidyā and Kalā, the forces of Karma, Time, Desire, ordinary perception and limited consciousness, all due to Māyā. One should transcend each group of tattvas that forms a veil, by meditation of them as being but a body, objective to him. This is Dhyāna and should be accompanied by Prāṇāyāma, Dhāraṇā, Pratyāharā and Samādhi. Prāṇāyāma leads to the dissolution of Prāṇā in the fire of Udāna in the central nādī. Dhāraṇā, steadying of vāyu in the parts of the body which correspond to the elements, is the means of the subjugation of the bhūtas. Pratayāhāra draws the chitta from the bhūtas and leads on to Samādhi, consciousness independent of objects. This gradual progress towards Samādhi is the characteristic of Āṇavopāya, but Shāmbhavopāya leads to the same goal without effort. There is the further inconvenience, when the three veils are crossed, of being surrounded by Māyā which is the root of these veils. Māyā is the mother of Siddhis, phenomenal powers, which lead one to another world of illusion (moha). Conquering these, one reaches illumination, sahajavidyā. Such a person, like the Vīrēsha or the one who has reached the shuddhatattva of the Shāmbhavopāya, feels himself one with the world. As a means of reaching the Shuddhatattva, a person who treads this path should think of the Ātmā as the actor, who in the various disguises of Jāgrat, Svapna and Suṣupti, plays on the stage of the mind (antarātmā), with the indriyas as audience. Finally, by controlling the Buddhi, he transcends it and reaches Independence. Parā Shakti, the seed of the universe, should now be meditated on ceaselessly, lest moha, illusion, should again envelope him. Gradually the uninterrupted bliss of Samādhi is reached, and the man obtains the Shāmbhavī stage, where he knows himself to be the knower and the known. Being permanently fixed in the Sahajavidyā, he transcends the sway of the Shaktis whose body is formed by Mantras and is released from rebirth. For this purpose, he should let the bliss of the Turya constantly drip like oil on his experience of Jāgrat, Svapna and Suṣupti. He should constantly seek being drowned in the bliss of Samādhi; when he returns therefrom to the ordinary consciousness, he well experience Samadarshana, *i.e.*, though experiencing limited consciousness, there will be an undercurrent of the knowledge of the identity of the seer and the seen. If in the stress of worldly life that undercurrent is broken and he fall back wholly into the ordinary, conditioned consciousness, he can recover Turya by turning his manas away from the objects of sense to the thought "I am Shiva." He then becomes equal to Shiva, Shīvatulya. The ordinary bodily functions of a Shiva-tulya are vrata; his talk is Japa; his knowledge of Ātmā is dāna, for his very presence inspires knowledge in others. The world is filled with his Shakti; he never slips from the consciousness of his being the knower. When he finally transcends pleasure and pain by recognizing that their play is outside his real self, he becomes a Kēvalī; even the relics of Karma do not then affect him. The jīva, the separated spirit, is destroyed, because desire that is the root of rebirth has been abandoned. He does not die yet, but he is not always aware of his body. When he uses his body, he descends to the Shivatulya state. When he discards it he finally crosses the ocean of Samsāra, steps into Paramapada, ever shining and full of bliss; he becomes what he always was—the Shivatattva, the one and only reality, the self-determined and blissful Shaṅkara.

Shiva-Sūtra-Vimarṣinī

PRELIMINARY NOTE

The Shiva-Sūtras "discovered" by Vasugupta is the last of a series of many anonymous works on the Shaiva Tantra known to us only by sundry quotations, *e.g.*, Vijñāna-bhairava, Mālinīvijaya, SvachhanDa, TimiroDghāta, etc. It is also the first of the series of works which expound the Kashmiri Shaiva School which was founded in the tenth century A.D., and which is yet alive. The first faint adumbrations of the Shaiva Tantra are found in the Taittirīya Yajur-Veda, but it developed into an organized system of beliefs and practices in South India in the earlier centuries of the Christian era, when the Shaiva as well as the Vaiṣṇava tantras became formidable rivals of the prevailing BauDDha, which had lost its pristine purity of an ethical code, and degenerated into an elaborate tantra. The Shaiva tantra travelled North and became the Lakulīsha Pāshupata of Gujarat and the Pratyabhijñā of Kashmir. Bhatta Kallata and Abhinava Gupta were the most famous of the successors of Vasugupta Kṣēmarāja, the pupil of Abhinava Gupta, wrote the commentaries—Shiva-Sūtra-Vimarṣinī, here translated. For a fuller account of the Kashmiri Shaiva and of its literature, *vide* my Outlines of Indian Philosophy, Chapter II.

Unmēṣa I–SHĀMBHAVOPĀYA

Whence the hosts of individual souls (Kṣētrajñas) rise veiled (in ignorance), where they obtain rest, what is truth, with whose activity the universe is filled, the principle of Spanda[1] which rises self-determined and blissful, is immortal and unsurpassed, that consciousness of Shaṅkara (which becomes) differentiated into two by cognition of relativity, is supreme.

Seeing that the existing commentaries have been vitiated by ignorance of tradition, I now comment correctly on the Shiva-Sūtras. There lived on Mahādēvagiri (Kailāsha?), the teacher, by name, Vasugupta, a great Maheshvara,[2] who rejected the teachings of Nāgabodhi[3] and other teachers of inferior schools (Darshanas); for, by the grace of Shivashakti, he possessed great devotion to Mahēshvara and always worshipped Shiva; and his heart was purified by following the paths of those who have mastered the Yoginis[4] of Paramēshvara. Once in a dream, he was illuminated with right knowledge by the grace of Parama Shiva, who was solicitous that the secret path should not be lost to the world of men, enveloped in the cognition of duality,[5] and revealed to him: "On a huge slab on this mountain, there is a secret (engraved). Take it and make it knwon to those who are fit for grace." On awakening, he searched for the stone and found one that turned upside down as soon as he touched it; (he, thereupon, knew that it was the stone that Shiva spoke of in his dream). The dream proved true and thence he got these Shiva-Sūtras, which are the epitome of the Shivopaniṣad.[6] Having obtained them, he published them to Bhatta Kallata and others of his disciples. He also embodied (the same teachings) in his Spandakārikā.[7] The Spanda Sūtras thus traditionally handed down have been explained by us in the Spandanirṇaya.[8] Here the Shiva-Sūtras are explained.

In the first Sūtra it is taught that consciousness is, in reality, but Shiva, the soul of the universe, in opposition to the theory that man and Īshvara are different beings.

I
Chaitanyam Ātmā : Chaitanyam is Ātmā

Since what is not cognized has no existence, the common characteristic of all objects is that of being manifested (chitikriyā) by the person that cognizes it. Chētana is he who makes manifest (chētayatē),[9] the master of all cognitive activity (jñānakriyā.) His nature is chaitanya, which thus denotes complete independence in the matter of cognitive activity. Such independence exists only in the Lord Parama-Shiva; for the activities of all beings down to those that do not seek Him, depend upon Him. Though He possesses endless characteristics,[10] *viz.*, Eternity of existence, Omnipresence, Formlessness, etc., yet these characteristics belong also to other beings; hence Independence, which alone is not found in others, has to be spoken of as His special characteristic. Hence this Independence is described, to the exclusion of other characteristics, by the abstract noun, *chaitanya.* This Independence is Ātmā; not any other category accepted by individualists,[11] one possessing a differentiated nature. If this individual soul conceived by the individualist to be different from the supreme soul, be other than Chaitanya, it would be characterised by unconsciousness and hence cannot be Ātmā. If it is of the nature of consciousness, it cannot be conceived as differentiated, for one consciousness cannot be cognized as separated from another consciousness on account of difference of space, time, or form. Though the ignorant do cognize such differences, wise men cannot accept (the theory) that consciousness can be differentiated. As the ātmā is thus pure consciousness, multiplicity cannot be ascribed to it. Differentiation cannot be predicated of it even when the defects (malas) which we are going to describe and which are opposed in nature to the atmā, attach themselves to it. Though at first the defects (malas) exist, they are extinguished on the attainment of liberation, and hence the doctrine of the multiplicity of souls cannot be maintained, for if the seeds of defects continue to exist at that stage, or if there is the least difference between the liberated Shiva and the beginningless Shiva,[12] they would still be unliberated (samsāris). Thus it has been proved that the theory of the multiplicity of ātmās it untenable, as said (in the Sūtra under comment).

(*Another explanation of the Sutra*).

For teaching those disciples who desire to enquire what is ātmā, he says that the ātmā is not what the Chārvāka, who does not accept the authority of the Vedas (Laukika), the Vedāntī,[13] who accepts the authority of the Vedas, the Yogāchāra, the Mādhyamika, etc., describe it to be, *viz.*, body, prāṇa, buddhi, shūnya (void), respectively, but it is chaitanya, as said in the Sūtra. For even when a man falsely conceives himself to be identical with his body, etc., that conception is illuminated (manifested) by the true one—the "consciousness[14] of I." As is said in the Mṛityujidbhattāraka: "It is taught in all the Shāstras that the essential nature of Paramātmā is devoid of all limiting conditions (upādhis), such consciousness is the nature of Ātmā." Also in Vijñānabhairava: "Consciousness is in all bodies, not special anywhere. Hence a man should conceive all beings as filled with it and thus become victor of samsāra (*i.e.* liberated)." This same teaching is contained in the two Kārikās (6, 7), of the Spanda, beginning with: "From whence this group of organs" and taught by the teacher (Vasugupta) to his disciples with reference to this Sūtra.

(*Third explanation.*) That which is called chaitanya is ātmā *i.e.*, svabhāva, Being, and as no adjective is used to qualify the word ātmā in the Sūtra, the ātmā of the whole universe which consists of real and unreal forms, is referred to. Now nothing which is never cognized can be said to have being. What is known is identical with the chit that is self-luminous; hence chaitanya is the same as ātmā. It is said in the Sūkṣmabhairava: "So long as knowers do not exist, how can there be the known, O dear one? The known and the knower are one substance. Hence matter does not exist as a separate principle (*lit.*, there is nothing impure)." This same teaching is contained in the Kārikās (28, 29), beginning with: "Because the Jīva is the all." As chaitanya is the nature of all beings, proofs are quite unfit to establish it, for they themselves have to be proved by self-luminous consciousness, and consciousness cannot be disproved (*lit.*, concealed) by any one, as it is always shining. It is said in the Tṛikahṛidaya: "Just as when a man tries to jump so as to get his feet where the shadow of his head lies, the shadow of his head moves off before his feet arrive there, similarly with the ray of the moon."[15]

With the same view, in the long passage of the Spanda, starting with: "Where established" and ending with "That is truly" (2-5), it is proved that consciousness, the principle of spanda, which is the nature of Shaṅkara, always self-luminous, is the Supreme Truth.

If the essence of the universe, which is made up of conscious and unconscious beings, be the consciousness of Paramashiva how can bondage arise? To answer this question, is composed the next Sūtra which is susceptible of two readings, according as 'a' is prefixed or not, as it is joined to the previous Sūtra or not:[16]

II

Jnānam Bandhaḥ : Knowledge is Bondage

Now as already said nothing more than the light of consciousness has existence; if so how can defect (mala) exist, or how can its suppression be possible? Thus the individualists question. In answer to this it is said in the Mālinīvijaya: "The ignorance (ajñāna) that causes the sprouting of samsāra is called mala;" and in the Sarvāchāra: "From ingnorance is the world bound; thence creation and destruction." As said in these quotations there is caused by Paramēshvara, by means of his wonder-working power (mahāmāyāshakti), in his own self, which is all-pervasive like the ākāsha, a limitation which extends to all beings, from those who have not turned to him for refuge up to those who have understood the nature of māyā; this limitation conceals his real nature which is illuminated by independence. It is the ignorance due to the want of the knowledge of identity of one's self with Shiva. It is the same as the āṇava,[17] which makes one think, "I am finite," the bondage whose nature is limited knowledge (jñāna). That nothing else can be taken as bondage is discussed fully by us in the Svacchandodyota[18] at the end of the fifth chapter in the discussion of Shrīdikṣa. The meaning of this Sūtra is referred to in the part of the Kārikā (9): "To him who has lost his independence by his own impurity." Now this jñāna, consciousness of limitation, which is also ajñāna of the nature of akhyāti, consisting of the attribution of materiality to the ātmā, is not alone bondage; but the ajñāna which consists in the ascription of the characteristics of ātmā to what is not ātmā, *viz*, body 8c., is the root-ignorance and is also bondage. This is referred to in Kārikā (46), beginning with: "The loss of the supreme essence of immortality." Thus have been described by means of this Sūtra the two kinds of aṇava-mala.

(1) What has been called chaitanya is characterized by independence; and though a conscious being, he does not exercise his independence and hence loses his wisdom and thinks: "I am finite." (This is the bondage of jñāna).

(2) Though characterized by independence, yet, while in the body, etc., he conceives what is not atma to be ātmā, this is the bondage of ajñāna. It is said in the Pratyabhijña (xiv. 3)[19]: "The loss of independence by the knower, and the loss of knowledge by the independent being, this is the double form of āṇava-mala, due to the suppression of his real nature."

Now is this aṇava-mala alone bondage? No. For it is said in the next Sūtra:

III

Yonivargaḥ Kalāsharīram : The Class of Yoni and Kalā-Bodied

The sentence is to be completed by supplying 'are bondage' from the previous Sūtra. Yoni is māyā, the cause of the universe. Its class (varga) is the group of principles from kalā[20] to the earth, which have māyā as their[21] cause, directly or indirectly, which originate bodies and worlds, and which are of limited activity. Such is māyā-mala.

That activity which manifests (kalayati) the specific form of each object is Kalā function; "kalā-bodied," means that which has activity as its nature, *i.e.,* karma. This is the bondage of Kārma-mala.

This also is referred to in (Kārika 9), "To him who is attached to action, having lost his independence through his impurity." This can be understood from our Spandanirṇaya. That these, *i.e.,* Kalā, etc., which are characterized by limited activity and which inhere in the same substratum as Āṇava-mala and envelope man constitute the (māyā) mala is stated in Svachchhanda: "Consciousness is obscured by (Aṇava) mala, surrounded by Kalā and Vidyā, coloured by Rāga, affected by Kāla, controlled again by Niyati, strengthened by the notion of being a Puruṣa, having Pradhāna as a dependent, connected with the three Guṇas, seated on Buddhi, surrounded by Ahamkāra, Manas, Jñānēndriyas, Karmēndriyas, Tanmātras and gross elements." That kārma-mala also surrounds man is stated in *Mālinivijaya:* "Karma, both good and bad, is associated with pleasure and pain." That Māyā-mala and Kārma-mala have Āṇava-mala as their substratum and are due to the limitation of knowledge is said in Pratyabhijñā (xiv. 3): "In (the āṇava mala) the individual consciousness, the Māyā-mala gives birth and experience and Kārma-mala, due to the ignorance of the actor."

Now it is considered how this triple mala, (1) Jñāna that is really ajñāna, (2) class of Yoni, (3) Kalā-bodied, causes bondage.

IV

Jñānādhiṣṭhānam Mātṛika : Mātṛikā is the Basis of Knowledge

This triple mala has been defined to be three states of consciousness: (1) consciousness of finiteness; (2)

cognition of the differentiated knowable; (3) deposits (vāsanā) of pleasure and pain, (*i.e.,* Karma). Its mother, the creatrix of the world is Mātṛikā, the unknown, of the form of letters from A to Kṣa. She associates the feelings of sorrow, astonishment, joy, desire, etc., with cognitions of the limited knowable, *(i.e.,* material objects), steady and unsteady states of consciousness, like "I am finite" (āṇava-mala)," "I am thin or fat" (māyā-mala), "I am an Agniṣṭoma-sacrificer" (kārma-mala), by endowing those cognitions with words that describe them. It is said in Timirodghāta: "Those Shaktis that are between Brahmārandhra and the Chiti, that hold the rope of Brahma,[22] the mistresses of the stations (pithas), most dreadful, again and again deceive men." She manifests the series of Shaktis, beginning from Brāhmī, which preside over varga, kalā, etc. She is described in the Agamas like Sarvavīra, as the maker of mantras, *i.e.,* one who arranges sounds in the proper order which makes them efficacious. She is embraced by the Shaktichakra, the totality of the energies of the universe, made up of Ambā, Jyēṣthā, Raudrī, and Vāmā.[23] She is the head of the Shaktis. On account of her influence the recognition of the interval between two consecutive states of consciousness becomes impossible and there is not even a momentary cessation of objective cognitions. Hence it is right to call this knowledge based on Mātṛikā, *i.e.,* cognitions which could be formulated in words, bondage.[24] This is referred to in Karikā (45), beginning with "To what is born of collections of sounds," and in Karikā (47), beginning with "The Shaktis are always bent on obscuring his nature."

Now the means of ending this bondage and the nature of the repose that is the goal is described.

V

Udyamo Bhairavaḥ : Udyama is Bhairava

Udyama is the flash of the Supreme Light[25] (Pratibhā), the sudden rise of pure consciousness which flows as unbroken meditation. It is the same as Shivashakti. It is Bhairava, becasue it fills (bhṛi) all the universe and because it swallows all faults due to the disturbance of illusions. It is taught in this Sūtra that as it developes the true nature of man which is Bhairava (universal consciousness), it is produced in those that are entirely devoted to introspective meditation.[26] It is said in Mālinivijaya, "That state which is produced even in those that have not cultivated thought, when enlightened by the Guru, is called Shāmbhava." In this quotation, 'enlightened by the Guru' has been explained by teachers to mean 'enlightened by the Guru, *i.e.*, himself.' It is also said in Svachchhanda: "O fair one, the case of the man that meditates on the bhairava form of himself and is steady therein, his mantras become efficacious." 'Meditation' referred to in this quotation is the continual determination of the mind inword. This is alluded to in Kārikā (4): "Unmēṣa is known to be that whence another thought arises when the mind is concentrated on one thought. This is to be understood from one's own experience."

Thus has been explained the means of becoming fixed in the suddenly risen supreme light and of thus becoming a Bhairava, which is the one means of ending the bondage of ignorance; now he says that on account of the strength of this meditation, even during Vyutthāna there continues the ceasing of duality. (Vyutthāna, Vyavahāra, ordinary action, the usual worldly activities; even when engaged in these his consciousness of universality is not destroyed. In the ordinary phrase, he is jīvanmukta).

VI

Shaktichakrasandhānē Vishvasamhāraḥ : On Union with Shaktichakra, The Destruction of the Universe

Bhairava has been explained to be characterized by the rise of supreme light. As he retains hold of the introspective attitude (meditation on the ātmā), he attains the unsurpassed supreme Shakti of independence; this power pervades the shakti-chakra of the universe, both gradually and all at once. Though this independence is described to transcend the gradual and simultaneous manifestation of the worlds, to be void, to be full, and to be both void and full, yet it is none of these things. It has already been shown that the manifestation of shakti-chakra in all stages of creation, *i.e.,* in all psychical experiences, from the ordinary cognition of objects, up to the final stage of the Supreme Knower, is but her sport with herself as the playground. On the regular meditation on the shakti-chakra which manifests as above, in the manner prescribed in the secret scriptures, is produced the destruction of the universe from Kālāgni to Rasakalā.[27] The universe composed of bodies and objects is burnt up in the fire of supreme consciousness. It is said in Bhārgashikhā: "He then swallows all these, death, time, the totality of kalās, all phenomena, all cognitions, all differences of one ātma and many ātmās." In Virāvalī, too: "Behold the funeral pyre in the body, which shines like the Kālānala, where all go to pralaya, all tattvas." In Mālinīvijaya, too, the same is described in a roundabout way: "This thing that cannot be described in words, has to be realized only by the mind. The state which all ultimately reach is called the Shākta." This has to be developed by devotion to the feet of the true guru and cannot be described fully. This same is referred to in the first as well as in the last Karikā, *viz.,* those beginning with "From whose waking and sleeping," and "When seated on unity", respectively.

Now it is said that to him whose universe is destroyed there exists no difference between Vyutthāna[28] and Samādhi.

VII

Jāgratsvapnasuṣuptabhēdē Turyābhogasambhavaḥ : The Bliss of the Fourth State is Produced in the Differences of Jāgrat, Svāpna, and Suṣūpti

In the various states of consciousness–Jāgrat, Svapna, and Suṣupti–which manifest themselves as different from each other and which are presently to be described, is born the bliss of the Fourth (Turya) state, described as Udyamo bhairavaḥ, which is of the nature of the illumination of all those states. The great Yogi who is spoken of as Bhairava, is eternally filled with the bliss of the Fourth state. Some read samvit in this Sūtra for sambhava and then the meaning is clear. This prevalence of the bliss of Turya in Jāgrat, etc., in the case of the great Yogi is described in Chandrajñāna: "Just as when the moon, like a flower, shines everywhere, it instantly rejoices the world with delightful things, so, O Dēvī, when the great Yogi wanders over the world, he everywhere causes joy to the world-picture from Avīchī to Shiva, by means of the moon of his jñāna." In the Spandā, this is referred to in Karika (3). "In the differences of Jāgrat, etc."

The three, Jāgrat, etc., are described in three Sūtras.

VIII

Jñānam Jāgrat

IX

Svapno Vikalpaḥ

X

Avivēko Māyā Sauṣuptam

Knowledge is *Jāgrat*: Fancy is Svapna. Ignorance, Māyā, is Suṣupti

Jāgrat is the experience a man gets, by means of the outer organs, *i.e.*, the organs of sensation, of objects which all people sense in common. Vikalpa, fancy, is born of mind alone (and deals with objects which other human beings do not sense). This is the state of Svapna; for it is chiefly concerned with these fancies. Avivēka, absence of distinction of one object from another, is ignorance. It is of the nature of Māyā, unconsciousness, the state of Suṣupti. In describing Suṣupti, the author has also described Māyā, which is to be abandoned. Thus by this description it is implied that there are three forms of each of the three states of Jāgrat, etc. Thus therein, *i.e.*, in Svapna, Jāgrat is the previous real experience that can generate a dream. The fancies connected with it constitute the Svapna. Want of discrimination of tattvas in the dream is the Suṣupti therein. In Suṣupti, these changes cannot be (easily) cognized; but when a desire to enter sleep is born, some state corresponding to Jāgrat previous to it is produced; its subsequent change into a state resembling a samskāra (unconscious mental modification) is the Svapna pertaining to Suṣupti.[29]

(Another interpretation)

According to the Yogīs, Jāgrat is the first consciousness of the concentration of the mind on an object; the conceptions flowing from thence, the various images (vikalpa) constitute Svapna; Samādhi, the non-cognition of the difference of the knower and the known is Suṣupti. This is taught by the words of this Sūtra. Hence in the old shāstras, the states due to the interconnexion of Jāgrat, etc., according to the Yogis are described as "Abuddha, Buddha, Prabuddha, Suprabuddha."[30]

The three states Jāgrat, etc., have thus been explained according to the ordinary and the yoga explanations. Now one who has destroyed his universe by union with shaktichakra, experiences the Turya filled with bliss and characterized by the consciousness of unity. He ascends the thread of Turya, enters the Turyātīta, the state beyond the fourth, already described as Chaitanya and becomes a—

XI

Tritayabhoktā Vīrēshaḥ : Virēsha, The Enjoyer of the Three

The three states of Jāgrat, etc., become filled with the bliss of the Fourth by reason of the union with shaktichakra. He who experiences the lessening of the samskāras (effects of the form of mental deposits) of the ordinary relative cognitions (the ordinary limited human consciousness) by the force of the new experience of the three states associated with the unceasing flow of bliss, is the Trityabhoktā. It is said: "He who knows both what is to be enjoyed in the three places (states), and who is called the enjoyer is not stained with mala though he enjoys." Hence he is the lord of the vīras, *i.e.,* the senses, which are capable of destroying the blissful, full, consciousness of a duality accompanying self-sovereignty. In the Scriptures he is called one who has acquired Shrimanthānubhairava.[31]

Thus it is taught that he who does not become a Virēsha but is the slave of the ordinary Jāgrat, etc., is but a pashu, a worldly man; and that even the Yogī who does not ascend this stream of bliss is not a Virēsha but a fool. This is also described in detail in Svachchhanda and other Shāstras. "The Yogi is one who by means of the yoga of svachchhanda, (independence) and by treading the path of svachchhanda reaches the state of svachchhanda and becomes equal to Svachchhanda (Shiva)." In the Spanda this is explained in Kārikā (17): "To him there is knowledge always fixed in the three states, etc."

Are there any subsidiary stages[32] to be reached by Yogīs when rising above the tattvas, by means of which the state above the tattvas can be seen? Yes, says the next Sūtra.

XII

Vismayo Yogabhūmikaḥ : Wonder (Characterises) the Stages of Yoga

When a man sees a new and peculiar thing he feels a sense of surprise. Similarly when a great Yogī cognizes, contemplates or enjoys the strange, excellent, and novel experiences[33] which flow into his consciousness, according as his mystic faculties are just opened, or staid, or fully expanded, he experiences a sense of surprise. This is frequently caused by his want of satisfaction in unbroken bliss. These are the stages leading to the union with supreme principle. They are the stages of rest in the ascent of the Yogī; they are regions of limited consciousness and not states when kanda, bindu, etc., are experienced. It is said in the Kulayukti: "When the Ātmā is born of itself by means of mystic practices, then the Ātmā in itself experiences wonder." This is referred to in Kārikā (11): "Who sees his own nature as the ruler and remains as if surprised, to him, how can this false show of the world exist."[34]

Of the Yoga who has reached this stage of yoga —

XIII

Ichchhācaktirumākumārī : Ichchhāshakti is Umā Kumāri

The desire of the Yogi who has reached the stage of the supreme Bhairava, is Shakti, Umā, the Supreme, the highest Goddess, whose nature is Independence. She is Kumāri, *i.e.*, devoted to the sport of creation and destruction of the universe. Kumāra means to sport, according to the Dhātupātha of Pāṇini (Kaṇdvādi). (Another interpretation). Ku, the state of māyā, the awakener of duality, mārayati, chokes its manifestation; Kumārī is one who has that characteristic. (Third interpretation.) Kumārī, a virgin, hence unfit to be an object of enjoyment; Umā manifests only as the enjoyer and not as an object of enjoyment. (Fourth interpretation). When Umā was a virgin she was not attached to anything and was always devoted to the worship of Mahēshvara which is the means of union with Him; so, too, is the Yogī's desire. The reading and explanation of my Guru is as above. Others read shaktitama for shaktirumā and explain that this Ichchhā is superior to Jñānā and Kriyā. This desire of the Yogī is not so gross as the desires of the worldly; but as it is of the same nature as Parāshakti, it is unobstructed. It is said in Svachchhanda: "That goddess has the names and forms of all other goddesses, is yet concealed by Yogamāyā; she is Kumārī, the author of the world." Also in Mṛityuñjayabhattāraka: "She, my Icchā, Parāshakti, potent, born of herself, is to be known as heat in fire, as the rays in the sun; that shakti is the cause of all the worlds." This same is otherwise referred to in Karikā (8): "He is not the inspirer of the prompting of desire; but by the force of his own Atmā a person becomes itself."

To one who has developed this Ichchha Shakti,

XIV

Dṛishyam Sharīram : The Visible World is the Body

Whatever is seen outside and inside, (*i.e.*, the objective world of material bodies and so-called subjective world of mental images, which together constitute the world of matter), all that is spoken of as 'This' and 'I,' appears to him as his body and not as different from him, on account of his great power, just as (the world appears) to Sadāshiva. His body, namely, the gross body, buddhi, prāṇa, and shūnya, is cognized by him as being as outside his real self as blue, etc., but does not as in the case of pashus,[35] manifest as the seer. Both in his body and outside, everywhere, his consciousness appears undifferentiated as the yolk of the pea-fowl. As said in Vijñānabhairava: "As waves of water, flames of fire, rays of the sun, these world-waves have started from me, the Bhairava." This is referred to in Kārikā (29): "Being enjoyer, he is always, everywhere, of the nature of the enjoyed."

It has been said that all the world is sensed by him as his body and all his bodies ending with the shūnya appear objective to him. This is not impossible; for,

XV

Hṛidayē Chittasanghattād Dṛshyasvāpadarshanam : From the Gathering Together of the Mind in the Heart, the Sight of the World and the Dream

The heart is the light of consciousness, the world is located there. "From the gathering of the mind" therein, means, imagining the mind to be one-pointed there. Thence one sees the world which consists of blue, gross body,[36] buddhi, prāṇa, and dream-world which contains none of these, but the shūnya body. The 'sight' spoken of here is the sensing of an object as one senses his body, and without the distinction of the perceiver and the perceived (which characterizes ordinary perception. The mind (chitta) which has entered the light of the Ātma sees the universe as clothed with it. It is said in Vijñānabhairava: "O fair one, he whose senses are concentrated in the ākāsha of his heart, who has reached the centre of the lotus-casket, whose mind is one-pointed (lit., engaged with no other), attains supreme bliss." Supreme bliss is the attainment of the lordship of the universe. With regard to the great Yogī who has attained the functioning of all the tattvas, it is said in Svachchhanda: 'He is seated equally in all bhūtas, bhāvas, tattvas and indriyas; he is in all moveable and immoveable, conscious and unconscious beings; he pervades all paths.'"[37] In the Spanda, too, (39), this is alluded to: "Thence, established in himself, is thus everywhere."

Now another means is explained.

XVI

Shuddhatattvasandhānād vā Apashushaktiḥ : Or the Becoming Devoid of Pashushakti by Meditation on Shuddhatattva

Shuddhatattva is the one called Paramashiva. When one meditates on the universe as being filled with Him, he transcends pashushakti, the source of bondage, and becomes the lord of the universe like Sadāshiva. It is said in Lakṣmikaulārṇava: "The experiences of steadiness (sthobha), etc., said to result from successful mystic initiation (dīkṣā), O Dēvī, are not equal to the sixteenth part of the results of meditation." Also in Vijñānabhairava: "One should meditate on all the body or the universe as filled with consciousness, at the same time, without interruption; then a supreme state is produced." This same is referred to in Kārikā (30): "He who has this cognition, who sees all the world to be a sport and is always in mystic contemplation (yukta), is certainly a jīvanmukta."

To him who has attained true knowledge (lit., is of the nature of knowledge),

XVII

Vitarka Ātmajñānam : Vitarka is Knowledge of Self

Vitarka is vichāra, the constant dwelling on the thought, "I am the ātmā of the universe, Shiva." This is ātmajñāna. It is said in Vijñānabhairava: "One that is firmly fixed in the idea 'I am omniscient, I am the actor in all actions, the Pervader, the Supreme Lord,' becomes Shiva." This is said in the Spanda (32): "This alone is the understanding of the Self (ātmano grahaḥ)." Here 'graha' is grahaṇa, apprehension, knowledge, of the Ātmā. This is but the sense of identity with Shiva, the ātmā of the universe. This meaning too is implied.

And to him,

XVIII

Lokānandah Samādhisūkham : The Bliss of Loka is the Ecstasy of Samādhi

Loka is that which is seen, the totality of the Object. Or loka is that which sees, the class of seers. It is said in Vijñānabhattāraka: "The cognition of the seer and the seen is common to all embodied beings; the speciality of Yogīs, however, is intentness on the connexion between the two." From intentness on the state where the difference between the cognizer and the cognized disappears, is born a bliss filled with wonder; this is the ecstasy of samādhi. It is said again therein: "Let one think of all the world or all the body as filled with the bliss of Self. At once he becomes filled with supreme bliss, by means of his own ātmā." This is taught in (Kārikā, 32): "This is the reaching of immortality."[38]

(*Another interpretation*).

The ecstasy of samādhi experienced by a man who is concentrated on his own self and looks on it as it is, developes not only bliss in himself, but also adds to the total bliss of the world.[39] This interpretation agrees with the quotation from Chandrajñāna (in commentary on Sūtra 7).

Now is described the wonderful power (vibhūti yoga) of this Yogī.

XIX

Shaktisandhane Sharirotpattiḥ : On the Meditation on Shakti, The Production of the Body

His shakti has been described in the Sūtra (13); "Ichchhāshaktir-umā kumārī." When he meditates on it he becomes steadily one with it. Then by means of its power whatever body he desires, that is produced. This is described in the passage of Mṛityuñjaya bhattāraka, beginning with—"Thence is produced the shakti devoid of objectivity (lakṣyahīna), without differentiations; she is called Ichchhā of the form of Jñāna, of the nature of Kriyā,"—and ending with "She is the womb of all the dēvas and all shaktis, manifold; the womb is of the nature of Agni and Soma; in it are all produced." The glory of meditation on shakti[40] is described in Lakṣmīkaularṇava in—"There is no mystic initiation (dikṣā) without meditation, nor the acquisition of powers (siddhi), nor mantras, nor the power of mantras, nor again success in yoga," and in other shlokas. This is explained in Kārikā (33): "When the creator at the instance of desire provides for the sake of embodied beings in the jāgrat state, things which are their heart's desire, by causing Soma and Sūrya to rise." (Commentary on this quotation.) "Embodied beings: Yogīs who have risen above the attractions of the body. "Things which are their heart's desire": Forms newly created. "Creator (Dhātṛ)": Mahēshvara." "Soma and Surya to rise": The shaktis are of the nature of prakāsha and ānanda, *i.e.*, light of consciousness and bliss, and make Soma and Sūrya flow. "Causing" that shakti or power which harmonises Soma and Sūrya, making them manifest objectively. The Independence in the state of Svapna, described in the shloka, that starts with 'Similarly in svapna too he attains desired objects" is illustrated (in Kārikā 34). This is explained by me in Spandanirṇaya.

Now it is said that others of the siddhis, as desired by him, are developed by the power of meditation on shakti.

XX

Bhūtasandhānabhū. Apṛthaktvavishvasaṅghattāḥ : Union with Bhūtas, Dissociation from Objects, Conjunction with the Universe

Bhūtas are objects like the body, prāṇa, bhāva, etc. Gratification in connection with them is bhūtasandhāna. Separation from the body, etc., in the cure of disease, etc., is bhūtapṛthaktva. Attaining to a true knowledge of the universe which is limited by space and time is vishvasaṅghatta. These powers are produced on the attainment of shakti already described. This is also described in the sections on sādhanas (practice) in all the Āgamas. This is explained in the Spanda (Kārikā 38): "One who attains it, though weak, engages himself in great actions; even so, though very hungry, he controls his hunger." (Illustration of bhūtasandhana). In Kārikā (40): "Disease is the thief of the body; its spread is due to ignorance. When that ignorance is destroyed by the rise of knowledge, how can that disease continue to exist, its cause being gone?" (Illustration of bhūtapṛthaktva). In Kārikā (36, 37): "Just as an indistinctly apprehended object appears more distinct when the mind is concentrated on it by the power of mind, so on the attainment of shakti, is soon manifested the truth in its own form and in its own place." (Illustration of vishvasaṅghatta.). Thus in the Vibhūtispanda[41] this is described with illustrations.

Now when without desiring the ordinary siddhis, he desires to experience universal consciousness, to him,

XXI

Shuddhavidyodayāt Cahkrēshatvasiddhiḥ : By the Rise of Shuddhavidyā, the Siddhi of the Lordship of the Chakras

When one meditates on shakti (*Cf.* Sūtra 19) with a desire to experience universal consciousness, Shuddavidyā *i.e.*, the consciousness, "I am all," rises and he becomes the lord of the shaktichakra of the universe, *i.e.*, becomes Mahēshvara. It is said in Svachchhanda: "It is the supreme knowledge, because there is none other; when he gets it he at once gets the supreme characteristics of omniscience, etc. It is the knowledge of the beginningless dharma, of paramātmā; it leads to the state of paramātmā, where the supreme light is manifested and he becomes fixed in it and reaches the state of Shiva." This is explained in Kārikā (43): "When with the desire of seeing all objects he pervades all of them, when there is no need of many words, he knows everything himself."

When he desires the bliss of Self alone,

XXII

Mahāhradānusandhānānmantravīryānubhavaḥ : On Attaining Mahāhrada, He Obtains Mantravīrya

When the light of consciousness (samvit), called Parā Bhattārikā, fills all the universe from Ichchhā-shakti (the beginning of the world) to the gross cognizable world, *i.e.*, when the Yogī senses all these at the same time, from it follows energy through Khēcharī and other chakras; it becomes clear, infinite, deep, etc., and is hence called mahāhrada (the great lake). By meditating on it, *i.e.*, thinking uninterruptedly, with inturned vision, of identity with it, is produced the efficacy of mantra, which consists of combination of sounds as will be described later.[42] This is[43] Parāhantā, manifesting as one's own self. This is described in Mālinīvijaya, in the shlokas beginning with "She, the shakti of the creator of the world," in which passage the shakti which fills the universe is shown to be of the form of Mātṛikāmālinī (one who has the mātṛikās as garland), because the world is of fifty different forms[44] from Ichchhā downwards; and after this passage the formation of mantras is described. Hence Mahāhrada is the supreme shakti. Hence it is right that the meditation on it should produce the efficacy of the mantras made of letters. This same is indirectly referred to in (the words), 'approaching that strength" (in Kārikā 26).

Beginning with defining chaitanya to be ātma, it was pointed out that bondage was due to ignorance of the independence of consciousness. Attainment of the state of bhairava which is udyama, puts a stop to bondage and fills the universe with bliss and gives all siddhis up to mantravīrya. Thus has been taught the first Unmeṣa (part), which gives an account of Shāmbhavopāya. Therein has also been described the nature of Shakti to indicate that Shakti exists in the nature of Shambhu. Blessed be it.

This is the description of Shāmbhavōpāya, the first chapter of the vṛtti, called Shiva-Sūtra-Vimarshnī.

Unmeṣa II–SHĀKTOPĀYA

Now is explained the Shāktopāya. It was declared at the end of the first Unmēṣa that Shakti is the development of power of Mantra. The author begins a new chapter with the nature of *mantra.*

I

Chittam Mantraḥ : Chittam is Mantra

Chitta is that by which the supreme truth is known (chētyatē), is meditated on (vimarshyatē). It is the knowledge consisting of the investigation of prāsāda,[45] praṇava, etc., accompanied by full consciousness.

Mantra[46] is that by which the nature of Paramēshvara mantryatē, *i.e.,* is meditated on by means of a secret mantra. Hence mantra is explained as 'man' and 'tra,' as 'manana' meditation and 'trāṇa,' protection, the ending of samsāra due to limited knowledge.

Again, mantra is not merely an aggregation of sounds, but the special chittam, the attainment of unity with the divinity behind a mantra by means of meditation. It is said in Vijñānottara: "The sounds that are uttered are not by themselves mantras. The proud gods and gandharvas were deceived by this false notion." It is said in Mantrasadbhāva: "The indestructible Shakti is regarded as the life of the mantras. Devoid of it, O fair-hipped one, they are as fruitless as an autumn cloud." And also in Shrīkaṇtha-samhitā: "A mantra separate from its mantri (the shakti behind it), cannot exist. Both flow from knowledge. They cannot exist apart from each other." In the Spanda, also, it is indirectly referred to in (Kārikā 27): "Those are Shiva-dharmis, who with the chitta devoted to Him."

And of it,

II

Prayatnaḥ Sādhakaḥ : Effort is the Means

The natural effort to fix permanently the energy that first rises from the desire to mediate on a mantra, defined as above, is the means that brings about the union of the practicer of the mantra and the deity of the mantra. It is said in Mantrasadbhāva: "When a bird in the sky sees a bit of meat, it soon picks it up with great natural speed, O dear one; thus the Yogīndra attracts manas, the bindu. Just as the arrow placed in the bow flies when shot with effort, so, O fair-hipped one, the bindu flies when pronounced." In another place, "The being of a mantra is the attraction of it." (Commentary on the quotations). Here 'Thus,' *i.e.,* by force of the natural effort, 'The Yogīndra attracts,' *i.e.,* he causes to attain supreme light, 'manas the bindu,' *i.e.,* the functioning mind. 'So the bindu,' *i.e.,* the supreme light, 'flies' *i.e.,* flows : by means of the natural effort of the pronunciation of the mantra.[47] In the Spanda (Kārikā 31): "This is the rise of the object of meditation in the mind of the meditator; this is the attainment of union with it by the practicer who desires it."

Now is described the mantra-vīrya, the efficacy, already referred to, of the mantra that is practised by the devotees.

III

Vidyā-sharīru-sattā mantra-rahasyam : The Secret of Mantra is the Nature of the Vidya-bodied

Vidyā is the consciousness of identity with the supreme. The vidyā-bodied is one whose form is vidyā, the lord who is the totality of sounds. His nature is the manifestation of the consciousness of being the Ego of, being identical with, the whole universe. This nature is the secret, the upaniṣad of the mantras. It is said in Mantrasadbhāva: "Mantras are all made of letters; these are the same as Shakti, O dear one; Shakti is the same as mātṛikā and she is the same as Shiva". In this book this subject, though very esoteric, is very fully expounded. The passage begins thus: "Those who delight in deceit and falsehood, and are unsteady and destitute of good deeds, do not know the Guru, the Dēva, nor the paths described in the Shāstras. Hence, O dēvī, I have rendered invisible the ways by which mantras may be made efficacious; the ordinary letters are worthless, on account of the concealment of mantra-vīrya". The passage about the mantras thus starts: "O dēvī, this mātṛika is possessed of supreme light; by her is all this universe filled, from Brahma down to the worlds. O dēvī worshipped of the gods, from there she spreads everywhere, as the letter 'A'[48] embraces every other letter. Thus will I explain to you clearly, so that you can understand it well." It then says: "This supreme, subtle Shakti is said to be nirāchāra (not functioning); she surrounds the bindu (drop of supreme light, *vide* com. on II. 2.) in the heart, and is like a sleeping serpent within. Sleeping there, O happy Umā, she is unconscious (lit., she does not think). Though she has within her womb the fourteen worlds, the sun, fire, the moon and the stars, yet she is as one fainted on account of poison. O faircomplexioned one, when she is churned by the bindu within, she awakes, with a great sound, and becomes conscious. O shakti-bodied, till then the churning is to be continued with forcible whirling. The sparks that are born first from this churning (bhēda) are excessively bright, when the subtle kalā, kuṇdalinī, is risen. The lordly bindu within the Shakti is of four rays (kalās). On account of the force of the churning, there is caused a straightening (the coiled one becomes straight), O dear one. She is called the jyēṣthā Shakti when she is between two bindus. Stirred by the bindu, the immortal coiled one becomes straight. She is then called rēkhinī (the straight); known as the three-footed, she goes then by the name of Raudrī. She is (also, called) Rodhinī, because she blocks (rudh) the path of mokṣa. Thus the one Parā Shakti becomes three-fold, of the form of a fragment of the moon, ambikā, and of the form of the half moon. On account of the conjunction and disjunction of these are born the nine classes of letters. Being united with these nine she becomes nine-fold. The dēvī then enters the five mantras, sadya, etc., in regular order. Hence she is known as five-fold, O mistress of the gods. She is said to be twelve-fold, because the vowels are twelve. She is divided fifty-fold, because she enters the letters 'A' to 'Kṣa.' When seated in the heart, she is said to be one-atomed; in the throat she is said to be two-atomed; so long as she is fixed in the root of the tongue, she is said to be three-atomed. The production of the letters is at the tip of the tongue, no doubt. This is the origin of sounds with which all moveable and immoveable things are pervaded."[49]

Thus the Mātṛikā Parā Vāk Shakti, belonging to the supreme Bhairava, flows in the forms of Jyēṣthā, Raudrī and Ambā, and thence all the sounds of the alphabet arise. This is the secret of the mantras which are formed by the combinations of these sounds and form the body of the great Goddess, the Vidyā-bodied being. Hence in all Āgamas the making of mantras is described with the description of Mātṛikāmālinī. As the Shiva-Sūtras constitute the essence of the secret Āgamas, we have said so much here to reconcile its teachings to those of the secret Āgamas. Hence we ought not to be condemned for prolixity. If in this discussion the reader discovers anything more to be known he has to go to his Guru for its elucidation. The meaning of this Sūtra is found in the Spanda (Kar. 26, 27), beginning "Having obtained the strength, mantras, &c."

This mantra-vīrya is the means of the attainment of the Mahāhrada already described; yet, in the case of those whose hearts have not, by the will of Īshvara, reached it, the mind attains ordinary acquisitions (mita-siddhi) when there is an incidental development of bindu, nāda, etc.

IV

Garbhē Chittavikāso Vishiṣtavidyā Svapnaḥ : In the Womb there is an Expansion of Chitta Ordinary Knowledge, Dream

'Womb' means Ignorance (akhyāti), Mahā-māyā. 'In the womb' means while under the influence of Mahā-Māyā (before the rise of Kuṇḍalinī Shakti, and the consequent expansion of consciousness). Even in this state there occurs mantra-siddhi, a limited expansion of consciousness and a consequent satisfaction of the mind. This is limited, impure consciousness, common to all men. So, too, his dream-consciousness (though expanded), but hallucination, based on differentiated cognition, manifoldness. It is said in Pātañjala (Yoga Sutras): "They are siddhis in vyutthāna, obstacles in Samādhi" (111, 38). This is explained in Spanda Kārikā 42: "From hence the bindu, from hence the nāda,[50] from hence form, from hence enjoyment, flow fast, causing agitation to the man in the body."

When suppressing the above ordinary acquisitions (mita siddhi) he sticks to the supreme state, the Yogi thence obtains,

V

Vidyā-Samutthānē Svābhāvikē Khēcharī Shivāvasthā : On The Natural Rise of Knowledge, Khēcharī, The Shiva-State

On the natural rise of knowledge already described, which is caused by the will of Īshvara and which suppresses the ordinary siddhis, is produced Khēcharī-mudrā. Khēchari is derived from 'Khē,' in the ākāsha (of consciousness), 'Charati; (what) moves. What kind of Khēcharī? The manifestation, the uprising of the bliss of the self, which is the avasthā of Shiva, the Lord of Chit. It is not that due to association with a body described in: "The Yogī bound in padmāsana,[51] must place the lord of the senses in the (lotus of the) navel; it must be led in the form of a staff up to the three ākāshas in the head; having fixed the mind there he must fill it soon with the three ākāshas; binding it there, the great Yogi moves along the ākāsha." But (the true Khēcharī) is of the nature of supreme consciousness as described in Tantrasadbhāva: "He reaches the supreme path by moving in the path of kula of all beings and meditating on all objects. This is known as Khēcharī." Thus have been taught (the true) mantra-vīrya and mudrā-vīrya; they are but the absorption into universal consciousness by ending all agitation due to the māyā of differentiated consciousness. It is said in Kulachūdāmaṇi: "There is bīja (seed) mantra of all beings; there is one mudrā, the Khēcharī; when these two are developed in a man he attains to the place of supreme peace." In the Spanda (Kārikā 9), too, mudrā-virya is contained in the description of mantra-vīrya. "When the agitation of the mind is quelled the supreme state is reached." Though this quotation refers to other subjects, it indirectly refers to the Khēchari described in (Kula) Chūdāmaṇi.

In the acquisition of mudrā and mantra vīrya,

VI

Gurur-Upāyaḥ : The Guru is the Means

The guru is the one that teaches, gṛiṇāti, the ultimate truth. He is the means, because he shows how they act. It is said in Mālinīvijaya: "The guru who shows the mantra-vīrya is equal to me (Shiva)." This is not referred to in Spanda as things like this are admitted by all. It can yet be obtained from the last Kārikā (52): "I salute the words of the Guru, who is the boat with which we cross the deep ocean of doubt, full of wonderful meanings."

(Another interpretation). Or, the Guru is the Shakti of Paramēshvara, the root of grace. It is said in Mālinīvijaya: "The mouth of the Guru is said to be the Shakti-chakra." In Trishirobhairava: "The Guru is the great shakti residing in the mouth of the Guru." It grants admittance to the disciple, hence it is the means.

Hence from the Guru full of grace,

VII

Mātṛikā-Chakra-Sambodhaḥ : The Knowledge of The Mātṛikā-Chakra

The sentence has to be completed by adding the words, "is secured to the disciple." It is indicated in Paratriṁshaka, etc. (The passage that follows is an exposition of the mātṛikā-chakra, but the sentence so ingeniously constructed that a word describing a Shakti corresponding to a letter begins with the same letters: as this feat cannot be exhibited in English the substance of the passage is given in tabular form.)

1. a, is the first ray of aham-vimarsha, consciousness of Ego; anuttarā, (supreme). She is Jñāna-shakti (Kula-Svarūpā).

2. ā, Ānanda rūpā, of the nature of bliss.

3,4. i, ī. She first illuminates the states of desire and lordship, ichchhā and īshāna.

5, 6. u, ū. She then exhibits the rise, unmēṣa, of knowledge and its obscuration, ūnatā, on account of the development of objective cognition.

7, 8. ṛ, l. These letters indicate the two functions of ichchhā-shakti, *viz.*, self-illumination and illuminating the world. Hence by illuminating the world with her own light she is immortal. But as the other seed-letters called sandhyakṣa (*viz.*, ē, ai, o, au), cannot be produced by merely illuminating the world.

9, ē. The three-angled seed-letter is produced by the union of anuttara, ānanda, and ichchhā.

10, o. Produced by the union of anuttara, ānanda, and unmēṣa. It embraces the kriyā-shakti.

11, 12. ai, au. The six-angled seed-letter and the trident seed letter. By the union of two seed-letters already described.

Thus all these are due to the union of the three shaktis, because in them kriyā-shakti is predominant, pervaded by jñāna-shakti and ichchhā-shakti.

13. ṅ. Bindu, indicates the knowledge of the oneness of the universe down to the physical world.

14. ḥ. Visarga, a double bindu, indicates the simultaneous inner and outer manifestation of the universe.

Thus the inner (subjective) states of consciousness, the (inner) world comes out of anuttara. This inner universe is that of the vowels; the outer, that of consonants.

In the outer creation, she evolves the whole universe ending with puruṣa (26 tattvas) corresponding to the 25 letters from ka to ma; ka-series from the shakti of a, cha-series from that of i, and so on from u, ṛ, l; each shakti of the vowel becomes five-fold and produces the five lower shaktis of the consonants.

The next four letters, ya, ra, la, va, are called antastha in Shikṣā, because they stand on puruṣa, within the kañchuka, niyati, etc. These four (*viz.*, niyati, kalā, rāga, vidyā) are called dhāraṇa, in the Vēdās, because they support the universe, standing on puruṣa, the knower.

The next four, sha, ṣa, sa, ha, are called ūṣma because they rise (unmiṣita) when difference is destroyed and identity is felt. Shakti then manifests in the form of these letters, of which the last, ha, is the letter of immortality.

After this she manifests the letter that is the life-seed prāṇa-bīja, kṣa. It is filled with the shakti of anuttara and with anāhata. Anuttara is a, hence its derivative, ka; anāhata is ha, which is sa, hence ṣa. Thus kṣa is a, ha, *i.e.,* aham which is the meaning and name of all this world, filled as it is in the light of the six adhvas. These six adhvas are said by Kṛiṣṇadāsa to be māyā, kalā, vidyā, rāga, kāla, niyati. Thus by taking the first and last letters, a and ha, together, we get aham, the world formed by the shaktis of Shiva, called anuttara and anāhata. This is the secret of ahamvimarsha, which is also mantravīrya. As said by Paramēṣṭhī Shrī Utpala Dēva, the venerable: "When prakāsha, (pure consciousness) is tranquillized in the self, it is called ahambhāva consciousness of self; it is called tranquillity (vishrānti), because then all desires are known. Its characteristics are independence, activity, and lordship." The secret of the mātṛikā so far explained has been shown to be the kūtabīji, kṣa, formed by the union of ka and ṣa, which proceed from the shaktis derived from anuttara. Thus has been expounded a very secret teaching.[52] (Now the translation is resumed).

The knowledge of the Mātṛikā-chakra causes one to enter his own nature which is a mass of the bliss of consciousness. Chakra is the totality of the Shak is above described, anuttara, ānanda, icchā, etc. Matṛikā is that which is referred to in—"There is no knowledge superior to that of the mātṛikā" (probably quoted from some late Upaniṣad). This knowledge has been but hinted at here. It is extensively described in Parātriṁshika-vivaraṇa Tantrāloka, etc., by my Guru (Abhinavagupta). It is said in Siddhāmṛita: "The Kuṇdalinī who is of the nature of consciousness is the life of all the seed-letters. From her is born the three, called Dhruva (same as anuttara), Ichchhā, Unmēṣa; then the letters from a, i, u, ṛ, l, up to visarga. From visarga, ka to ma fivefold, outer and inner, in the heart, is sound, in the cosmos. The bindu works from the heart to the head. Mantras without the letters a to ma are useless as the autumn cloud. The characteristics of a to ma should be learnt from the Guru who is learned, who is bhairava, who is godlike, and is to be reverenced like myself (Shiva). Then knowing it, one sees everything as mantra." In the Spanda this is indirectly shown in the passage beginning with "This Shakti of Shiva is tinged by Kriyā. It influences pashus. Left free it creates the bondage of Samsāra. Rightly understood it helps one to attain Siddhi."

To the man who has acquired a knowledge of mātṛkāchakra,

VIII

Sharīram Haviḥ : The Body is the Sacrificial Food

The body, gross, subtle, etc., which is wrongly regarded by all as the cognizer, is the sacrificial food which the great Yogīs throw in the fire of consciousness; for when this wrong notion of the body is gone, they are always absorbed in pure consciousness. It is said in Vijñānabhairava: "When in the fire in the temple of the great Void, elements, organs and objects with the manas are sacrificed, that is homa (sacrifice); chētana (consciousness) is the sacrificial ladle (sruk)." In Timirodghāta: "O Dēvī, one flies in the hall of the sky by eating the limbs of one who is dear, who is a friend, a relative, a giver, who is most dear." This means that the function of the body in subserving cognition should be put an end to. In Gītā, too: "Others burn the functions of all sense-organs and the activities of prāṇa in the fire of the yoga of self-control, illuminated by the light of knowledge" (iv. 27). In Spanda, it is referred to in (Kārikā 9), "When the agitation is quelled, that is the final stage." Here 'agitation' is the identification of 'I' with the body, etc., as explained by Bhatta Kallata in the Vṛitti.

To him,

IX

Jnānam Annam : Knowledge is Food

The knowledge that is described as bondage (1.2) is the food of Yogīs, because it is eaten, swallowed, as discussed already (Comm. on i. 6)? "He then swallows all these, death, time, the totality of kalās, all phenomena, all cognitions, all differences of one ātmā and many ātmās." (Another interpretation). Or, the knowledge which consists in the meditation on one's own nature is his food, it being the cause of the peace of the self because it produces full satisfaction. In Vijñāna-bhairava, it is said: "What rises day after day, when fixed in one stage (yukti), is the consciousness of fulness, the bliss due to that fulness." 'Yukti' is here the knowledge of 112 stages. It is explained in Kārikā (44): "He will stand everywhere enlightened."[53]

In the case of the man who is not always in equilibrium, and though wise, is proud of having reached the stage of equilibrium.

X

Vidyāsamhārē Tadutthasvapnadarshanam : When Knowledge is Destroyed, the Vision of Dream Born Therefrom

On the destruction, *i.e.*, sinking of shuddhavidyā, which is the extensive wisdom already described, all traces of that wisdom are gradually destroyed and there rise therefrom visions (svapna), *i.e.*, manifestations of illusory worlds filled with consciousness of differentiation. In Mālinīvijaya, in the passage beginning with: "When Shankara is not graceful the Guru does not teach this; even if he should teach it, the teaching becomes fruitless," it is said that even if the fruit of the teaching is acquired the Vināyakas make one who is careless become addicted to evanescent pleasures. In Spanda (Kārikā, 35), the same is taught in: "Otherwise, from its own natuıe, creation starts of itself, as in the case of the worldly man do the states of jāgrat and svapna." It is thus taught that the Yogī should be always bent on Shuddhavidyā. As said in Shrī Pūrva: "One should fix his desire on the Supreme and not be attached to these." Also, in Spanda (Karika, 21), "Hence, always endeavouring to discriminate the Spandatattva, being always careful, one soon reaches the truth."

Thus from beginning with 'Chittam mantraḥ,' he has discussed the Shāktopāya, whose chief characteristic is the acquisition of Mantra-vīrya and Mudrā-vīrya, and which is described in the Āgamas thus: "Thinking of the thing that cannot be named one reaches the stage that is called Shākta," and has ended it with 'Vidyāsamhārē taduttha-svapna-darshanam,' with regard to one who is proud of having reached equilibrium, thus opening the way for the Āṇavopāya, which is related to it. May it be blessed.

This is the description of Shāktopāya, the second chapter of the Vṛitti, called Shiva-Sūtra-Vimarshinī.

Unmēṣa III - ĀNĀVOPĀYA

Now with a view to explain Āṇavopāya, he describes the nature of aṇu.

I

Ātmā Chittam : Ātmā is Chitta

Chitta includes buddhi, ahaṅkāra, and manas, whose constant functions are adhyavasāya, etc., as it is filled with the deposits of the experience (vāsanā) of objects. It atati *i.e.*, wanders in wombs, by taking up the activities of sattva, etc., and by ignorance of its own nature as being pure consciousness; hence it is ātmā, the aṇu. But atana, wandering, does not really belong to him, for he is of the sole nature of consciousness. Hence Ātmā has already been described by 'Chaitanyam ātmā (*i.e.*), intended to describe his real nature. Now however it is defined so as to indicate its state as aṇu, characterized by decreased knowledge. Thus there is no contradiction between the earlier and later definitions.

Of this ātmā who is chītta by nature and yet aṇu,

II

Jñānam Bandhaḥ : Knowledge is Bondage

That knowledge which is of the form of the experiences of pleasure, pain, indifference, illusion, certainty, etc., and of the nature of relative consciousness appropriate to them, is bondage. Bound by it he enters samsāra. It is said in Mantrasadbhāva: "Those who are under the influence of sattva, rajas, and tamas are knowers of guṇas. The embodied man wanders thus and goes from place to place." It is also said: "Imprisoned in puryaṣtaka, which rises from the tanmātṛas and stays in buddhi, ahaṅkāra and manas, the dependent one undergoes the experiences born from it and from objects. Thence he wanders in samsāra." Thus in Spanda (Karika, 49, 50), in reference to a previous passage: "Now we explain the cause of samsāra and pralaya".[54]

Now it is said in Vijñāna-bhairava: "All knowledge illuminates; the ātmā, too, is the illuminator; on account of the identity of these two, the knower shines with knowledge. "Since knowledge is illumination, how then can it be bondage? This is true, if by the grace of Paramashiva, we obtain Pratyabhijñā[55] (recognition of this fact); but when by His Māyāshakti, this knowledge is not born,

III

Kalādīnām Tattvānām Avivēko Māyā : The Ignorance with Regard to the Tattvas Beginning from Kalā, is Māyā

'The tattvas beginning from kalā are those from kalā to kṣiti, characterized by limited power and divided into kañchuka,[56] puryaṣtaka, and sthūladēha. 'Ignorance with regard to' them is the notion that they are identical with the man though they are really distinct from him. This is Māyā, full of the ignorance of the tattvas, the (differentiated) universe. It is said in Mantrasadbhāva: "He whose consciousness is shaken by kalā, sees objects by vidyā, is coloured by rāga is associated with the buddhi and other organs, is subjected to the bondage of māyā, dharma and adharma are attached to it. Fixed in these, the man that deserves bondage is bound." In the Spanda, too, this is indirectly referred to in (20): "These of unenlightened buddhi endeavour to conceal their nature."

Hence for its ending,

IV

Sharīrē Samhāraḥ Kalānām : In the Body, the Destruction of the Kalās

'The body'[57] is (1) the gross body made of the gross elements, (2) the subtle body of Puryaṣtaka, (3) the supreme body that ends with mokṣa. Therein reside the kālas, parts, *i.e.,* taṭtvas from the earth to Shiva. One should destroy them by meditating on each as being dissolved in its cause, or by thinking of them as forming the body (and as being objecting to the man). In Vijñāna-bhairava: "Let him think of all, in order, in the forms of the world, objects, etc., in the states of gross, subtle, and supreme till in the end they are dissolved in the manas.' Again: "Let him think of his city as burnt up in the kālāgni, born of kāla. In the end the illumination called shānta is born." Such and similar teaching is found in all Āgamas. Hence dhyāna, etc., have been called āṇava in the early shāstras, as in: "That state is well called āṇava, which is produced by the different kinds of uchchāra (breathing), karaṇa (mudras), dhyāna (as defined in the Yoga-Sūtras, the sixth of the eight aṇgas of yoga), varṇa (mantras), and sthāna (chakras)." As this deals with the gross (āṅavopāya), it is not explained in the Spanda, which deals with the shāktopāya alone. What in this work leads ultimately to the Shāktopāya, we have tried and shall try to show its agreement with the Spanda."[58]

Having thus described the āṇavopāya called dhyāna, he now describes prāṇāyāma, dhāraṇā, pratyāhāra, and samādhi, which are allied to it.

V

Nādīsamhāra-Bhūtajaya-Bhūtakaivalya-Bhūtaprithaktvāni : The Stoppage of the Nādīs, the Conquest of the Elements, the Separation from the Elements, and the Independence of the Elements

These have to be meditated on by the Yogīs. The nādīs are tubes which carry prāṇa, apāna, etc. Their stoppage (prāṇāyāma) causes their dissolution in one place, *i.e.*, the central tube of the fire of udāna, by joining prāṇa and apāna to it. It is said in Svachchhanda: "Fill by means of the right; empty by means of left. This is the purification of the nādīs and the path that leads to mokṣa. Prāṇāyāma is said to be threefold, emptying, filling, and control. The outer prāṇāyāma (control of the breath) is common to all beings. The inner[59] again is threefold; fill by means of the inner; making kumbhaka by them (controlling the inner breath), without motion, the inner are done."

The conquest of the elements is the subjection of the elements, earth, etc., by dhāranā.[60] It is said in Svachchhanda: "The dhāraṇā (steadying) of air (vāyu) in the thumb and the toe, of fire in the middle of the navel, of the earth in the throat, of water in the ghatikā, of the ākāsha in the head is known to be the cause of all the siddhis."

The separation from the elements is pratyāharaṇa, the drawing away of the chitta from them. It is said: "When the prāṇa which moves in the heart and the manas which runs after sense-objects are confined in the navel, it is prāṇāyāma, the fourth, called suprashānta." By the independence of the elements is meant pure, independent consciousness, apart from them. It is said: "Having regularly broken up all that ends with unmana and given them up by the means already described, O dēvī, he attains independence." What has been previously described as "union with bhūtas, dissociation from bhūtas, conjunction with the universe" (i. 20), is acquired without effort by one who is engaged in Shāmbhavopāya, but this is acquired with effort by means of Āṇavopāya. This is the difference between them.

This siddhi, which is called tattvarūpa, coming from purification of the body, purification of the elements, prāṇāyāma, pratyāhāra, dhāraṇā, dhyāna, and samādhi, is due to being enveloped by illusion and not knowledge of truth. This is taught in the next Sūtra.

VI
Mohāvaraṇāt Siddhiḥ : Siddhi is from Being Surrounded by Illusion (Moha)

Moha is māyā, what causes loss of knowledge. From being surrounded by it and from a gradual development of dhāraṇā, etc., already described, is produced the siddhi which consists in the enjoyment of that māyā-tattva, but not the knowledge of the supreme tattva. It is said in Lakṣmī-kaulārṇava: "The self-born lord is devoid of birth and samsāra; the deluded one does not see the changeless supreme abodes without beginning and end, peaceful, revealed in all beings."

In the case of one whose moha is destroyed, "following the middle prāṇa, then the interior prāṇa and apāna, taking hold of jñāna-shakti, one should reach steadiness (āsana) in it." Udāna is jñāna-shakti, because all characteristics of life are drowned in it. "Giving up the characteristics of the gross (body), *i.e.*, prāṇa, etc., then the interior subtle (one), is reached the spanda, the supreme, that is beyond the subtle. Hence this is called prāṇāyama; thence one does not slip. Giving up the functions of guṇas, sound, etc., which are experienced by the mind, one should enter the supreme abode by his mind. This is called pratyāhāra, which cuts off the noose of Samsāra. Transcending the qualities of buddhi, meditating on that which is beyond meditation, the supreme, the pervading, one should meditate on the self-luminous; this the wise know to be dhyāna. That by which one is always steadied in the supreme ātmā is called dharaṇā, that puts an end to the noose of Samsāra. Regarding equally the elements in oneself, and in others, and in the world, the samādhi (fixity-in) the (thought): "I am Shiva, I am secondless,' is the supreme state. Thus as described in Mṛityujidbhattāraka, even by dhāraṇā, etc., is produced entry into the supreme tattva; but not partial siddhi (mitasiddhi). This is said in the next Sūtra.

VII

Mohajayādanantābhogātsahajavidya Jayaḥ : By Endless Extension of the Conquest of Moha, is Produced the Acquisition of Sahajavidyā

Moha is māyā, the bondage which is ignorance and ends with the ending of samsāra. By its being thoroughly conquered, *i.e.,* till all the samskāras (deposits of karma) are entirely destroyed, is born the acquisition of sahajavidyā, described as "the knowledge of beginningless dharma etc., (*vide* comm. on i, 21). As already said even āṇavopāya leads to shāktopāya. Thus in Svachchhanda, in the passage which begins with: "O fair one, the web of bondage, endless, ending with shamana," and which closes with—"After transcending cognition caused by bondage, one cognizes the essence; this is ātmavyāpti; shivavyāpti is other than this; when one thinks of the objects possessing the qualities of omnipotence, etc., as operative, that is shiva-vyāpti, the cause of chaitanya," it is said that by the conquest of the moha that leads to ātmavyāpti is attained the unmana, which is shivavyāpti the sahajavidyā. It is said there—"Giving up thence the ātmatattva, one should join the vidyatattva. This is known as unmana, determined by the manas. From determination, the knowledge called unmana gradually rises and becomes established once for all. It is the supreme vidyā because there is none better. When one gets it, he at once gets the supreme characteristics of omniscience, etc. It explains the beginningless dharma, teaches of the paramātmā, and leads to the state of paramātmā, hence it is vidyā, and established in it, he manifests the light supreme the supreme cause."

Thus having attained the sahajavidyā, he becomes,

VIII

Jāgrat Dvitīyakaraḥ : Wakeful, Having the Second as His Rays

If one who has attained the shuddhavidyā takes care to keep steady in it, he becomes one who has as his rays the world, which is 'the second' to ahantā (I-ness), pūrṇavimarsha (unlimited consciousness), which is called idantā (this-ness), and which manifests itself as the known. It means the universe appears to him as his rays. As said in Vijñānabhairava: "Wherever through the senses the consciousness of the Lord manifests itself, that has the nature of tanmātra, hence it becomes dissolved in consciousness, hence it becomes filled." Also in Sarvamangala: "Two things are mentioned, shakti and the possessor of shakti; shaktis are to Him all the world, and Mahēshvara is the possessor of shakti."[61]

Of him who is thus bent upon investigating his own nature,

IX

Nartaka Ātmā : The Ātma is an Actor

The ātmā is an actor, *i.e.,* manifests on himself as substratum, various disguises, *e.g.*, jāgrat, etc., his activity being a sport, rooted on his own real nature concealed within himself. It is said in Naishvāsadēvīmahēshvaranartaka, vii, in the stotra by Dēvī, "Thou art in one aspect the ātmā within, (in another) the actor, protector of kosha."[62] By Bhatta Nārāyaṇa, too, "Hara, what other poet is capable of beginning and ending the drama of the three lokas, sown with so many central ideas and so many catastrophes". In Pratyabhijñā-Sūtra, which is the Upaniṣad of the Āgamas, it is said—"He who carries on the drama of the Universe (samsāra), who is awake when the world sleeps (pralaya) is the one, Paramēshvara."

Of this actor in the world-drama, the stage where he puts on the disguise, *i.e.,* the seat of bondage, is next described.

X

Rango-Antarātmā : The Stage is the Ātmā Within

'Raṅga' is the stage where he rajyātē, *i.e.,* paints or enjoys, playing the drama of the world.[63] The place where he puts on the disguise is the antarātmā, the ātmā within, which is characterized by contraction and manifestation, which depends on shūnya or prāṇa (in svapna or in jāgrat respectively), and is anterior to the body of puryaṣṭaka, and which is jīva. Remaining there, he shows the world-drama in accordance with the functions of his manas (his karaṇa, instrument). It is said in Svachchhanda: "Wandering in all wombs, on account of union with puryaṣṭaka, he is called antarātmā, this is the true doctrine."

Of him who plays on the stage of the antaratmā,

XI

Prēkṣākāṇīndriyāṇi : The Organs of Sense are the Audience

The eyes and other sense-organs of the Yogī introspectively see his real nature, filled with the pleasure of manifesting the drama of the world. They attain, by the excellence of the play, the state where distinctions are abolished and they are filled with the appreciation of the wonderful play. It is said in the Shruti (Katha Up. iv. I) "The self-existent Lord pierced holes outwards; hence one sees outward, not at the ātmā within; some wise one sees the ātmā within with inturned eyes enjoying immortality."[64]

To him,

XII

Dhivashāt Sattvasiddhiḥ : By Control of Dhī, Sattvasiddhi is Produced

Dhī is intellect fit for investigating the nature of the tattvas. By its control is manifested the sattva, whose nature is light, which is subtle internal activity. Even in a dramatic performance the appreciation of subtle gesture is attained by clearness of intellect.

By attaining this sattva of illumination,

XIII

Siddhaḥ Svatantrabhāvaḥ : Independence is Attained

Independence is the conquest of all the universe and is characterized by spontaneous knowledge and power of action. It is said by Shrīnātha: "One should obtain the power of independence for oneself; she is Shrī, Kālī, Parāyalā." In the Svachchhanda: "All things known as tattvas, bhūtas, and mantravarṇas, are always under his control, by always contemplating on Shiva."

To him the power of independence is,

XIV

Yathā Tatra Tathānyatra : As There, So Otherwhere

As in the body where the Yogī's self is manifested, so in all other places where he concentrates himself, that power is produced. It is said in Svachchhanda: "He lives always independent and independent and independent." In the Spanda, too, (Kārikā 7): "That tattva has to be examined with effort and earnestness, whence his independence, unopposed and omnipotent."

However, he should not be careless, but,

XV

Bījāvadhānam : Concentration on the Seed

Add, 'should be made.' Bīja, the seed, is the cause of the universe, of the nature of illumination, Parāshakti. It is said in Mṛityujidbhattāraka: "She is the womb of the gods and of the manifold shaktis, the womb of the nature of Agni and Soma; hence all things start." On the seed, that is the Parāshakti, avadhāna, *i.e.*, frequent concentration of the chitta, should be made.

While he is thus,

XVI

Asanasthaḥ Sukham Hradē Nimajjati : Being Steadied, He Easily Bathes in the Tank

Established in āsana, *i.e.*, concentrated on ātmā alone by the power of Shakti, after having given up the difficult practices of dhyāna and dhāraṇā, supreme and non-supreme, if one always meditates by means of introspection on. It, he, easily, without difficulty (bathes in the tank of bliss). This tank is the supreme ocean of immortality, which is the source whence this universe flows like a flood, and which consists of svachchha and uchchhalata. In it he bathes, sinks the limitation of knowledge due to his body, etc., and becomes one with it. It is said in Mṛityujidbhattāraka: "Do not direct contemplation above, nor below, nor again in the middle, nor at all, before or behind, nor in the two sides, nor again in what is inside the body, nor contemplate on any things outside. Do not direct your mind on the akāsha, nor look below. Let there be no closing of the eyelids, nor any binding of the eyes; do not concentrate on a support, or the unsupported or the supported; nor on the indriyās, nor on the bhūtas, sound, touch, taste, etc. Having given up these, fixed in samādhi, he should be full of it. This is called the supreme state of Shiva, the paramātmā. That is the stage without ābhāsa (reflection, reflected consciousness); having reached this stage, one never returns."[65]

Thus by beginning the ānavopāya, *i.e.*, nādisamhāra, etc., conquest of illusion is attained; thence is produced Shāktabala, whose nature is Shuddhavidyā. On attaining it the Yogī reaches Shāmbhavī stage, whose nature is hrada, the supreme amṛita, made by himself. Then he,

XVII

Svamātrānirmāṇām Āpādayati : He Creates the Manifestation of a Part of Himself

Svamātrā is the part of his ātmā, engaged in meditation of the nature of chaitanya, chidrasa; he manifests the illumination of knowledge and the known with the light of himself. It is said in Svachchhanda: "That is gross, O dear one, because it is under the gross upādhi; the one is divided into gross and subtle." Also in the Pratyabhijñā: "Hence he makes himself the known, but not what is already the known." In the Āgama, too, the same is said: "Dear one, he who knows water and ice, by means of the Āgamas, from the mouth of the Guru, has nothing further to do; to him there is no further rebirth." The same is explained in the Spanda "He whose consciousness sees thus all the world as a play and is always fixed in samādhi is certainly a jīvanmukta."

Now it is said that to him who possesses objects, qualities, and bodies created by his own power, there is no bondage of birth, etc., whatsoever.

XVIII

Vidyāvināshē Janmavināshaḥ : When Vidyā is Permanent Birth Ceases

When the sahajavidyā already described is manifested always, there results the destruction of birth, *i.e.*, union with bodies and organs, under the compulsion of karma and producing ignorance and full of pain. It is said in Shrīkantha: "Having given up the world, which is characterized by acquisition and abandonment, which is mobile, from Shiva to the earth, filled with formed and formless, *e.g.*, grass, leaf, stone, etc., and meditating on all as filled by Shiva, he never again attains birth." Also in Svachchhanda:

"Having known the supreme pure nirvāṇa that is got from the teaching of the Guru, one is released; then he is not reborn after death." In Mṛityujit, too: "Having seen by the divine path of yoga the state beyond the three tattvas (ātmātattva, vidyātattva, and shivatattva), eternal, changeless, permanent, one is not again reborn."

When the characteristics of Shuddhavidya are drowned, of him,

XIX

Kavargādiṣu Mahēshvaryādyaḥ Pashumātaraḥ : In the Ka-class etc., Mahēshvarī and other Mothers of the Pashus[66] Become the Ruling Deities, has to be Added to Complete the Sentence

It is said in Mālinivijaya: "O dēvī, she who is called Shakti and who inheres in the lord of the world, takes on the desire-nature of him who desires to create. Hear how she attains multiplicity, though one. That by which, in this universe, one knows for certain a thing to be this and not otherwise, is called jñānashakti. When the idea is born, 'Let this thing be thus,' the power which makes it so at that moment is called kriyā-shākti. Though she is thus of two forms, Īshvarī, when conjoined to objects, becomes, like Chintāmaṇi, of endless forms. Therein she attains motherhood (mātṛibhāva), becomes divided two-fold, nine-fold, and fifty-fold; she thus becomes mālinī (a series). Two-fold, as bīja and yoni; bīja are the vowels; yoni from ka, etc., divided into nine classes (varga). The bīja mantra is Shiva, and Yoni is known to be Shakti. By division into eight classes (vargas), the eight shaktis (varga), Mahēshvari, etc., come. By division into 50 letters she is fifty-fold. She attains that number, being called by the names of Rudras." Thus she, Pārameshvarī, Parā Vāk, the flowing Ichchhā-shakti, takes on the forms of jñāna-shakti, kriyā-shakti, of bīja, yonivarga, and vargya, etc., becomes the mātṛikā, of the forms of the letters from 'a' to 'kṣa' and of the names, Shiva, Shakti, Mahēshvarī, etc. In certain and uncertain cognition (avikalpaka-savikalpaka-samvēdanam) of all knowers, she is in the form of the cognition within and in the forms of subtle and audible sounds makes that cognition known. By being the ruling goddesses of varga, vargya, etc., she manifests the feelings of wonder, joy, fear, desire, aversion, etc. She then conceals her real nature of chidghana (unlimited consciousness, massive sentiency), unlimited, independent, and attains a limited, dependent, embodied state. It is said in Timirodghāta: "Seated between brahmarandhra and chiti, embracing the rope of Brahma, the mistresses of the pīthas, most terrible, again and again, deceive (men)." This has already been quoted. It has already been said that 'mātṛikā is based on knowledge' (i. 4). The special point brought out here is that though one has attained the tattvas, yet by ignorance he is deceived by Mahēshvarī and other mistresses of pashus by means of the knowledge of mere sounds.

Hence the Yogī should in all circumstances be careful to see that the Shuddhavidyā attained by the means already described, should not be lost. This is said in the next Sūtra.

XX

Triṣu Chaturtham Tailavad Āsēchyam : In the Three the Fourth should be Dropped Like Oil

In the three states of jāgrat, etc., the fourth state, that wherein Shuddhavidyā manifests and the bliss of turīya is experienced, should be dropped, drop by drop, like oil. Just as oil gradually spreads over a surface, so should the turīya experience which is first had at the extreme points (the beginning and end of every state of consciousness) in jāgrat, etc., be extended to the middle, so that the state of consciousness might be immersed in it.

In the Sūtra, "The experience of turīya in jāgrat, svapna, and suṣupti" (i. 7), has been described the nature of turīya as causing the flow of its own essence in jāgrat and other stages, when one is steady in udyama and union with shakti-chakra. In "Vīrēcha the enjoyer of the three" (i. 11), has been shown the ending of jāgrat, etc., by means of hathapāka following the shāmbhāvopāya. In this Sūtra, it is taught that the essence of turīya should be dropped on jāgrat and other states so as to spread like a leaf. This is how this Sūtra differs from the rest.

Now the means of securing this is explained.

XXI

Magnaḥ Svachittēna Praviṣhēt : Being Drowned, Let Him Enter by Means of His Own Chitta

In accordance with the passage in Mṛityujidbhattāraka, which begins with "Whence, having given up the gross prāṇa, then the subtle, interior prāṇa, one attains the supreme that is above the subtle," and ends with, "He should enter with his mind," one should give up the gross methods of prāṇāyāma, dhyāna, dhāraṇā, etc., and enter (the supreme) by means of the certain knowledge born of introspective meditation with his mind. Then he should destroy his perception of his body, prāṇa, etc., by drowning himself in the bliss that flows from his consciousness. It is said in Svachchhaṇda: "Giving up the mental activities, direct yourself to pure consciousness. Then the pashu is released from the ocean of samsāra and becomes Shiva." Also in Vijñānabhairava: "When the four, *viz.*, mental function, chētanā, shakti, ātmā, O dear one, are weakened, the body becomes bhairava." This same (very obscure verse) is explained in the stotra, called jñānagarbha: "O mother, having ended all mental functions from all sides, given up the dependence due to the functioning of the (sense and action) organs by your favour, one experiences that supreme state, which is devoid of stupor and spreads nectar-like and never-changing bliss." This is by my Mahāguru.

When a man who has entered paramapada again deviates into worldly things, he will have,

XXII

Prāṇasamachāre Samadarshanam : The Cognition of Sameness on the Slow Motion of Praṇa

When the prāṇa purified by shakti of pure consciousness, is in slow motion on account of the steadiness inside of the developed shakti, he experiences, in all states, the one bliss of pure consciousness. It is said in Ānandabhairava: "Giving up the worldly life, one should follow the advaita, the giver of mukti, common to all the gods, in all castes and āshramas. He who sees all objects alike is released from all bonds." Hence it is said in Pratyabhijñā: "The real nature of the universe is attained by those who have risen above contracted knowledge of outside objects, even though buddhi and prāṇa act in them."

He who having attained steadiness in the introspective turīya state, does go on to the state beyond the turīya (turīyātīta), but remains satisfied with the wonderful experiences of the beginning and end of the turīya state,

XXIII

Madhyē' Varaprasavaḥ : In the Middle is Born a Non-excellent State

In the case of one who gives himself up to the enjoyment of the delight of the beginning and end of the turīya state, is born in the middle a non-excellent, ignoble vyutthāna. In accordance with the Sūtra, "Vidyāsamhārē tadutthasvapnadarshanam," (ii. 10), he is always deceived.

It is said in Mālinī-vijaya "Although one has the vāsanā of the turīya state yet if he is careless, Vināyakas make him have temporary enjoyments. Therefore he who wishes to rise high should not mingle with wordly things."

Even if such a state is born, if he again drops the middle state by fixity in turīya,—

XXIV

Mātrāsvapratyayasandhānē Naṣṭasya Punarutthānam : On the Non-union of Cognition to Objects, the Loss is Recovered

Union of cognition to things is described in Mālinīvijaya: "What is seen by the eyes, what is manifested by speech, what the manas thinks on, what buddhi knows, what are felt to be the actions of the Ego, what is the known, what is not, this has to be sought with effort." In the non-excellent state of mind already described, one meditates always on the 'pure consciousness' "I am all this universe." The lost steadiness in turīya is recovered, and the Yogī gets unity with it. This is said in Svachchhanda, in the passage beginning with "The manas of Yogīs is forcibly shaken," and ending with "If one is fixed in the consciousness of being the knower and is full all round, his manas is unshaken in all states wherever the manas goes, all that is to be taken as the knower; if all is filled with Shiva where will the manas go when it is shaken?" and "In all things and objects of sense, whatever we perceive, there is nothing which is not Shiva."

The Yogī who has reached this supreme state,

XXV

Shivatulyo Jāyatē : Becomes Equal to Shiva

By force of meditation on turīya, he reaches the state beyond turīya, filled with pure, independent, bliss of consciousness, equal to Shiva. He is equal to Shiva because he has not yet lost his body. When he loses it he becomes Shiva himself. This is said in Kālikākrama: "Hence, having learnt from the Guru's lips the yoga, eternal and without doubt, one should by steady meditation imagine himself to be filled with Him. When he attains equality with Him, he becomes Lord Bhairava."

Yet, as it is said, "From whence this, that verily from experience," the body which exists for transcending the experience already come (*i.e.*, prārabdha) cannot be discarded. This is said in

XXVI

Sharīravṛittir Vratam : The Bodily Functions are Worship

Whatever bodily functions are exercised by the Yogī who has been said to be equal to Shiva, and who is meditating on the thought, 'I am Shiva,' are acts of worship, consisting of a constant investigation of his own nature. This has to be done by him always. Thus in Svachchhanda: "As the flame of a burning fire[67] is seen (to end in empty) space, so the ātmā has to be dissolved in the prāṇa of the body. It is said here that union with Shiva is possible only to him who is in a body and prāṇa. To him no other worship than being in a body is useful. It is said in Trikasāra: "That wise man who keeps always in the mudrās that arise from the body, is called the bearer of mudrās; others are bearers of bones." Also, in Kulapañchāshikā: "The rays (shaktis) speak to him who has an unmanifested liṅga; they do not approach one who has a (manifested) liṅga, for they are hidden."

Of such a man,

XXVII
Kathā Japah : His Talk is Japa

As he is filled with consciousness of Ego always, as explained in Svachchhanda: "I am verily the supreme Hamsa, Shiva, the supreme cause," if one should be filled with the great mantra of the consciousness of Ego, described in Kālikākrama: "The consciousness of him, the god of gods, of the form of supreme knowledge, is Shakti, omniscient, full of wisdom," his talk is japa, of the nature of the constant repetition of the consciousness of ātmā. It is said in Vijñānabhairava: "What is again and again conceived in the supreme thought, that is japa, having its own sound; this is what is fit to be recited as mantra." Again "By saying Sa he goes out (of his body in his breath); By saying Ha he re-enters; hence the jīva constantly repeats the mantra, 'hamsa' 'hamsa,' always; six hundred times during the day and twenty-one thousand times during the night; this easy japa has been ordained by the Dēvī, difficult to fools."

Now is described the conduct of one who possesses this japa and vrata.

XXVIII
Dānam Ātmajnānam : Knowledge of Ātmā is Gift

His realization of the ātmā which has been said to be chaitanya, is his dāna (charitable gift ordained on all as a daily duty). (Now the commentator gives a few fanciful derivations and explanations of dānam).

Dīyatē, means 'khaṇdyatē,' 'there is cut off all cognition of difference;' 'dāyate,' shodhyate, 'the nature of māya is made clear;' 'dīyatē' is rakṣyatē, and rakṣyatē means lakṣyatē, *i.e.* the characteristics of Shivātmā obtained by him are well described. Or, again, 'dīyate,' 'what is given' is dānam; knowledge of self is given by him to his disciples. It is said: "The Yogīndras, who follow steadily the kulāchāra, save one from the wide ocean of samsāra by their mere sight or touch."

When one becomes equal to Shiva, as said (in iii. 25) and masters the true Shaktichakra by steady vrata (iii. 26), japa (iii. 27), and charyā (iii. 28), he alone becomes a fit teacher of disciples. This is explained in the next Sūtra.

XXIX

Yo'vipastho Jnāhētushcha : And Who is Avipa is the Cause of Knowledge

Avipa is what protects (pāti), pashus (avīn, pashūn), the Shaktichakram, Mahēshvarī, etc., as described in the Sūtra, 'Kavargādiṣu māhēshvaryādyaḥ pashumātaraḥ" (iii. 19). He who is in the state of avipa, who manifests his independence on account of the knowledge of his own greatness, is the cause of knowledge. 'The cause of knowledge' means one that is able to teach others by means of jñānashakti. How can others, who are not masters of themselves being subject to shaktichakra, teach disciples? The word 'who' (yaḥ) in the Sūtra requires the introduction of 'he' (saḥ) in it. 'Cha' in the Sutra means 'hi' verily. As the person in avipa is the cause of the rise of knowledge in others, it has been well said, "Dānamātmajñānam" (iii. 28).

Others following the Nirukta rule (that by which each letter of a sūtra is supposed to stand for the word of which it is the initial or final letter), interpret this Sūtra as follows: 'Yo' is yogīndra; 'vi' is vijñāna; 'pa' is pada; 'stha' is the last syllable of padastha; jñā is jñātā; 'he' is hēyaḥ; 'tu' is tuchchhatā; visarga is the visargashakti; 'cha' represents what is not said, *i.e.*, the actor (kartā); and explain this Sūtra to mean that the Yogīndra who has reached the stage of realization of the ātmā by means of vimarshashakti (discriminating inquiry) is to be known as the knower and actor. To him all evil appears insipid, unfit to be pursued.

This interpretation does not appeal to us, as the making up of the meaning is not elegant, as if each Sūtra were to be interpreted thus, thousand-fold interpretations could be made out.

To him,

XXX

Svashaktiprashayo'sya Vishvam : The World is Filled with His Own Shakti

Because he is said equal to Shiva, "His shaktis (are) all the world," as described in the Vedas; the universe is filled with his own shakti. The world is the manifestation of the kriyāshakti, which flows from his own pure consciousness. It is said in Mṛityujit: "O, Dēvī, since the manifold knowable world is filled with knowledge and since this knowledge is the salvation (trāṇam) of the limited beings (niyantṛita), it is called nētra." Also is Kālikākrama: "Knowledge manifests itself, inside and outside, in various forms; objects have no existential value (sattā) unless they are cognized; hence the world is of the nature of knowledge (has an ideal existence). No concept (bhāva, mental image) can be apprehended without cognition; hence it has been proved that the world is of the nature of consciousness. By the distinction of what is and what is not, joined to command and countermand (in the sphere of duty), by the power of conceiving images, the known has the same nature as knowledge. As cognition is simultaneous, the knower and the known are one."[68]

Not only is it at the time of creation the world is the manifestation of his own shakti, but also after (creation).

XXXI
Sthitilayau : Maintenance and Destruction are Filled with His Own Shakti

"Maintenance" (sthiti) is the manifestation as object for a short time (the moment of cognition) of the world as that result of kriyāshakti, for the benefit of cognizers. "Destruction" (laya) is the cessation of cognition by the cognizer who is consciousness. Both are filled with his shakti. This cognized world is identical with consciousness both during cognition during its cessation. Otherwise cognition would be impossible. Hence in Kālikākrama: "By the discrimination of what is and is not, etc.," (quoted in the commentary on the last Sūtra), sthiti and laya are described. So it is said: "He who sees all as pure, knowledge without (a separate) substratum, (but) identical with consciousness of self, is a mukta (liberated soul), though yet living in a body, no doubt."

Now it might be thought that in the different states of creation, maintenance, and destruction, the ātmā becomes differentiated. In reply it is said,

XXXII

Tatpravṛittāvapyanirāsaḥ Samvtiṛibhāvāt : Even When They Prevail, He Will Not Slip from the State of Knower

Even when the states of creation, etc., rise, this Yogī does not slip from being always engaged in the consciousness of the turīya. For when there is a change from that state there is no light of consciousness. It is said there: "When the experience of knowledge is destroyed, the real nature of the Yogī is not lost, for it is without origin or destruction; therefore the ending of knowledge is not real. Origin and destruction are falsely attributed to knowledge; How can one say that is lost which by nature is indestructible?" This same is described in Spanda-Kārikā: "There are two states described, action and agent; action is finite, but agentship is deathless." Again, "Effort to do an action ceases, (but not the result of it); when the effort ends, the man thinks I am lost. That which is gained by introspective meditation is the basis of omniscience; that can never be lost, for if so all other things would be lost."

To this Yogī,

XXXIII

Sukhaduḥkhayorbahirmānanam : The Contemplation of Pleasure and Pain as Outside

He recognizes pleasure and pain born from contact with the world (lit., the known), as outside him, as objective to him, as blue, etc., and does not regard them as subjective experiences as the ordinary man of the world does. The latter cognizes everything as subjective experience (with the light of egoism), as said in "Sashaktiprachayo'sya vishvam" iii. 30), not as predestined pleasure and pain, etc. How could the Yogī who has transcended the consciousness of puryaṣṭaka be affected by pleasure and pain? So it is said in Pratyabhijñāsūtra-vimarshinī: "Pleasure and pain (though due to true causes) do not exist for those who have transcended the stage of cognizers of relative consciousness and reached the stage when they know the absolute truth; or (it may be) pleasure and pain do not rise in them, for the causes of pleasure, etc., do not exist for them. Then the birth of true knowledge takes place." Hence it is said in Spanda : "Where there is no pain, no pleasure, no cognized, no cognizer, no ignorance, That truly exists."

Because to the Yogī who has transcended the consciousness limited by puryaṣtaka there is no connection with pleasure and pain.

XXXIV

Tadvimuktastu Kēvalī : Who has Given It Up is 'Alone'

He who has absolutely transcended pleasure and pain, whose mind is not affected even by the relics (samskāra) of them is kēvalī, knower of pure consciousness. It is said in Kalikākrama: "The Yogī who has destroyed the great delusion of duality which is largely determined by the experience of pleasure and pain, gets the fruits of yoga." The word 'tu' shows his distinction from him who is going to be described in the next Sutra.

Tu in the next Sūtra indicates the same.

XXXV

Mohapratisamhatastu Karmātmā : He Who is Overcome by Delusion is Verily Karmātmā

One who is weighted with moha, *i.e.*, ignorance, and is hence affected by pleasure and pain is karmātma, always stained by good and evil. It is said there (Kālikākrama):

'Pleasant and painful things are experienced on account of that which being surrounded by ignorance, and impelled by changes, soon creates all beings from Shiva downwards. From unhappy experiences supreme misery results."

When such a karmātmā gains his own independence, on account of the grace of the invincible Mahēshashakti, (he obtains)

XXXVI

Bhēdatiraskāre Sargāntarakarmatvam : When Difference is Ended, Creatorship of Another Creation

On the destruction of differentiated consciousness, which is characterized by love of body, prāṇa, etc., as himself, and is experienced by Sakalas, Pralayākalas, etc., *i.e.*, when limited consciousness is driven away by the rise of absolute consciousness, are gradually developed the powers of Mantra, Mantrēshvara, and Mantramahēshvara, the ability to create another universe by mere desire. Thus in Svachchhanda: "By three-fold japa, one becomes equal to svachchhanda" it is said that equality to svachchhanda is attributed to one who has transcended limitations. Then: "He becomes the terror and refuge of Brahmā, Viṣṇu, Indra and other gods, the lords of Siddhas, Daityas and serpents, he also becomes the giver of blessings and curses. He destroys the pride of time, fells mountains."

This is not impossible, for

XXXVII

Kāraṇashaktiḥ Svatōnubhāvāt : On Account of His Own Prowess, Kāraṇashakti

By his prowess, both in the desire (of waking moments and of) dream, kāraṇashakti, the power of creating extraordinary things, is proved to exist in the ātmā. With this in view it is said in Pratyabhijñā: "Hence from conception and illumination according to his desires, jñāna and kriyā are clearly proved to exist in all living beings." Just so; if he meditates with great fervour, then is born the power to create all common things at will. It is said in the Tattvagarbha: "When they shine self-manifested, skilful, weakness is banished when they are engaged in great deeds, and their desires become like kalpaka trees."

As has been said, the nature of the knower who is pure consciousness is Independence, kāraṇashakti, the fourth (state of) ātmā, which relights its nature destroyed by māyāshakti.

XXXVIII

Tripādadyānuprāṇanam : Living at the Roots of the Three States

The three states are called (1) creation, (2) maintenance, (3) destruction, which are respectively (1) preparation to birth, (2) embracing it, and (3) relapsation of it; their source, the turīya, a mass of bliss, though enveloped by māyāshakti on account of the development of the three, during the moments of enjoyment, shines like lightning. Though it rises but for a moment during those moments, it has to be dwelt on, by following the differences of introspective meditation; by the living power the relighting of the living is to be done. It is said in the Vijñānabhairava: "The state of the Bhairava has for its aim the following of the directions of the changes of bliss, it is experienced within, and is full; its pure and omnipresent nature has to be truly known;" beginning with this passage, it is further said: "That bliss of brahmatattva, which is born on union with shakti and ends on being filled with shakti is called svārtha. O Dēvēshi, from clear memory of the pleasures of woman, licking, churning, one is drowned in bliss, even in the absence of power. From the mere memory of the pleasure enjoyed when a great bliss befalls a man or when he sees a relative whom he has not seen for a long time, one becomes filled with bliss and is drowned in it. From the bliss arising from the pleasures of eating and drinking, one should infer the nature of Bhairava and become filled with bliss. To the Yogī who is filled with the bliss other than that experienced from singing and other enjoyments and who is master of his mind, is born that nature (of Bhairava)." Thus have the means been shown. The same is also shown in the passage beginning, "Whether very angry or highly pleased, hesitating to move or running, whatever state a man is in, that state contains spanda" and ending with "The enlightened one is without limitation." This has been fully explained by me in Spandanirṇaya. In Sūtra, "Triṣu chaturtham" (iii. 20), it was said that the turīya has to be experienced in jāgrat, etc. In this Sūtra it is taught that it has to be experienced in the beginning, middle and end of all states, indirectly described as creation, maintenance and destruction.

One should not rest content with the interpenetration of the three states with the fourth, during introspective meditation alone; but

XXXIX

Chittasthitivachchharīrakaraṇabāhyēṣu : As in the Fixed Chitta, so in the Body, Organs and the Object, the Accompaniment of the Three States by the Fourth should be Practised

As when the chitta is fixed during introspective meditation, one should practise the interpenetration of the three states by the turīya, so too during the (ordinary) conscious life of body, organs and the object, though the mind is turned outward, one should be fixed in the inner consciousness and accompany it (the conscious life) with it (the fourth), gradually getting stronger in each stage. It is said in Vijñānabhairava: "One should think of all the universe or of his body as being filled with bliss; he is at once filled with supreme bliss on account of his immortality." Thus while the power of blissful Independence becomes manifest in all states he becomes able to create according to his desires.

When he does not experience this cognition accompanied by the interior fourth state, then on account of the āṇavamala, which is the consciousness 'I am finite,' due to his consciousness of the body,

XL

Abhilāṣād Bahirgatiḥ Samvāhyasya : He Goes Out on Account of the Desire of the Samvāhya (Jiva)

Samvāhya is one that is led from womb to womb with kañçhuka, inner organ, outer organs, tanmātras and bhūtas, dominated by the shaktichakra. He is the pashu, of the kind called karmātmā. Of him it is said in Svachchhanda, "Verily, desire is in his case mala;" he is always intent on objects, because of desire, on account of the āṇavamala of the nature of the consciousness of finiteness, he never cares for the practice of introspective meditation. It is said in Kālikākrama: "Pleasant and painful things are experienced on account of that which, being surrounded by ignorance and impelled by changes, soon creates all beings from Shiva downwards. From unhappy experience supreme misery results. Imagining all sorts of unrealities they suffer in hell, etc.; their faults burn them as easily as bamboos in fire. They suffer from ignorance on account of thoughts full of māyā; these men attain bodies full of māyā, the seat of sorrow."

When on account of being touched with the shakti of Paramēshvara, he is enlightened and recognizes his real nature then desire dies and his mind is not outward-turned, but is self-gratified.

XLI

Tādārūdhapramitēstatkṣayājjīvasamkṣayaḥ : From the Consciousness Being Fixed in It from the Destruction of It (Desire), the Jīva is Destroyed

"Fixed in it." It is the ātmā, the knower, already described, the fourth state. One fixed on it "it, is one that possesses the knowledge that rises from a cognition of it." "The destruction of it" is (the destruction of) desire; therefrom results the ending of the jīva, the samvāhya, who experiences the consciousness of puryaṣtaka; he manifests the consciousness of chit. As said there: "Just as the objects seen in a dream are not seen when one awakes from sleep, so by the Yogī who is in meditation, is the world not seen." As also: "The Yogī who has put a stop to good and bad actions, reached the interior consciousness, destroyed the supreme and non-supreme series of mental images by the consciousness of unity, is eternally satisfied with himself, and is devoted to the destruction of time; he is the Yogi that is the experiencer of kaivalya and gets the state of nirvāṇa." The experiencer of kaivalya is one who is not overcome by the senses, tanmātras, etc.

Now when the jīva is destroyed, he loses his body; even when he awakes he is not always aware of his body. How then can he get any cognition through it? This is answered in the next Sūtra.

XLII

Bhurakanchukī Tadavimukto Bhūyaḥ Patisamaḥ Paraḥ: Enveloped by Bhūtas, then, Released, Frequently Becomes Equal to Pati, Supreme

'Then', when desire is ended, when the love of the consciousness limited by puryaṣtaka is dropped, he is 'enveloped by bhūtas,' *i.e.*, the elements which produce the body are like an envelope, like a cover, separate from him, not touching the seat of ahaṅkāra. So he is released, he is an enjoyer of nirvāṇa; hence he becomes frequently filled with the nature of Paramēshvara, an absolute consciousness. Hence he is supreme, full. As said in the Sūtra, "Sharīravṛittir vratam" (iii. 26), though yet in a body, as (water) on a leaf, he is untouched by the bodily consciousness. It is said in Kularatnamālā: "When the great guru teaches him well, there is no doubt left in him; that very moment he becomes free, just where he stands. What more need be said of the wise who are entirely devoted to the supreme Brahma? The Yogī who remains free even for a moment liberates all men." Also in Mṛityujit: "What truth is seen even in the twinkling of the eye liberates a man from rebirth." In the Kulasāra, too: "Behold the greatness of truth, O fair one, from mere hearing it one becomes free."

Now it is said that this state of being loosely enveloped by bhūta is not ended all at once.

XLIII

Naisargikaḥ Prāṇasambandhaḥ: Connection with the Prāṇa is Natural

'Naisargikaḥ,' from nisarga, the nature of ātmā, *i.e.* Independence. The blessed lady, Pure Consciousness, desiring to manifest the wonders of the universe, attains first the consciousness of limitation, then the state of knower, *i.e.*, the consciousness of the limited Universe which is prāṇana, and then manifests as universe, the known. Hence her connection with Prāṇa is first produced from Independence and is natural. In Vājasanēya: "She, Shakti, supreme, subtle, pervasive, pure, auspicious, mother of Shaktichakra, supreme bliss, of the nature of immortality, Mahāghorēshvari, Chaṇḍā, the author of creation, and destruction, forcibly drags time, the bearer of three, three-fold;" thus is Pure consciousness described as the bearer of three-fold prāṇa, Soma, Sūrya and Agni; the manifester of three-fold time, past, present, and future. It is said in Svachchhanda: "Prāṇa is the Being with prāṇa; prāṇa is for breathing in. She seated in the heart is of breathing beings and always fills them with prāṇa;" Prāṇa is said to be ha, flowing spontaneously, of the shape of a plough, hence it is of the nature of Svachchhanda Bhattāraka; hence it fills in (the lungs) and empties and is said to be the author of creation and destruction. Thus it has been said that the connection with prāṇa is natural. The same has been called by Bhatta Kallata the power of the operative cause, called, prāṇa—"Being Consciousness at first, she then becomes prāṇa,"—in his Tattvārthachintāmaṇi.

Now, the connection with prāṇa having been proved to be natural, it is going to be shown that one who controls it, and continues to meditate on its innermost part is the greatest in the world.

XLIV

Nāsikāntarmadhyasamyamāt Kimatra Savyāpasavyasauṣumnēṣu : After Control of the Middle of the Interior of the Nāsikā in the Right, Left and Middle Nāīdis, What More Need be Done?

Of all the nādis the three most important are savya, apasavya and sāuṣumṇa, otherwise termed right, left and middle nādīs. Nāsikā means the prāṇashakti which moves crookedly among these nādīs. Nāsikā is derived from "nasatē" meaning (it) moves crookedly. That which is in its (Nāsika's) middle is Samvit or the internal consciousness. There is nothing more to be said after fixing the internal sight on 'Vimarṣa' which is inside samvit, which is at the core of everything, and is therefore the most important, and which is described as follows in Kālikākrama: "Vimarṣa is the highest shakti of him who is above the Dēvās and who is the supreme knowledge in form. Vimarṣa is all knowing and is illuminated by "*jñāna.*" This shines brilliantly in all states and is called Nirvyutthāna, the best samādhi. It is said in Vijñānabhairava: "The cognition of the seer and the seen is common to all embodied beings; the speciality of Yogīs, however, is intentness on the connection between the two."

Relating the fruits of yoga enjoyed by such a man (he the author) finishes the book.

XLV
Bhūyaḥ Syāt Pratiniryāṇam :
There will be Relapsation Again

This universe which is derived from the form of chaitanya will completely relapse into chaitanya, since the consciousness of difference will be gone. That is to say, the Yogī settled in the best yoga will assume again his own form of chaitanya. It is said in Svachchhanda, "Oh Dēvī, settling in 'unmana' one must fix the self there. If the ātmā is thus fixed it becomes That." It is again said in it—"A stick set on fire when well burnt does not resume its former state of wood, so ātmā is removed from Samsāra. He who is free from mala, karma, kalā etc. is released from misery and does not suffer though remaining in mala, &c., for he becomes supremely pure." What the author means by 'bhūyaḥ syāt' is that Shivatva is not a thing to be newly achieved by the Yogī:

it is nature. Māyāshakti creates vikalpa or consciousness of difference. On account of the evil effects of this he is not able to know the shining shivatva (in him). By following the methods described above he will have cognition of shivatvam. May it prosper!

This is the description of Āṇavopāya, the third chapter of the Vṛitti called Shiva-Sūtra-Vimarṣinī.

(Closing Verses)

1. This Vṛitti explains the secrets of Shaiva religion and is so written as to harmonise Agamas and Spandakārikās.

2. Good people in order to shake off samsāra should enjoy this Shiva-Sūtra-Vimarṣinī which is filled with the sweet fresh nectar oozing from the explanation of the Secrets of Shiva.

3. It creates interest in the indifferent: it develops the mind well: by tasting this death, old age, birth and other dangers can be averted as by tasting nectar.

4. Man being surrounded by the body, prāṇa, pleasure, &c., cannot cognize his ātmā's chaitanya which is of the nature of Mahēshvara. He who knows this universe as the foam surrounding the milky ocean of knowledge is alone said to be Shiva himself.

5. Cross the ocean of Samsāra soon. Firmly step into paramapada, ever shining and full of felicity. Carefully think over the Shivasūtra full of secrets. It develops knowledge backed by sound reasonings.

6. Thus ends Shiva-Śūtra-Vimarṣinī composed by Rājānaka Kṣēmarāja serving under Mahāmāhēshvara Rājānaka Shrīmad Abhinava Gupta.

NOTES

Introduction

1. Ordinarily, though wrongly, called Nạkulīsha.

Shiva-Sūtra-Vimarṣinī

1. Spanda is the ultimate principle of the universe according to this system. It is otherwise Shiva, the unlimited Pure *Ego,* the one and only substratum of the universe, whose motion or activity is the cause of the differentiation of the knower and the known, of cognition and action, which are the ultimate factors of the world-process.

2. Māhēshvara is the name given to the followers of the schools which accept the Shaiva Āgamas as revelation, and worship Shiva as the supreme Deity. They are more popularly called Shaivas.

3. Nāgabodhi was a popular teacher of later Buddhism, when it became overladen with the practices of the Tāntrikās, and the Shaiva and Vaiṣṇava Tantras became its great competitors for popular favour. He is mentioned in Hall's *Catalogue,* 196.

4. Yoginīs are troops of goddesses, who, among other things, preside over the whirls of occult energy, called chakras, in the subtle body.

5. So long as men are enveloped in a cognition of duality they cannot gain true knowledge and hence cannot attain to a release from rebirth.

6. Shivopaniṣad may mean either an Upaniṣad of that name of which we know nothing, or merely Shiva's secret teachings.

7. Published with the commentary called Spandapradīpikā of Utpala, by Pandit Vāman Shāstri Islampurkar, vol. XII of the

Viziayanagaram Sanskrit Series. It is noteworthy that in different recensions, as also by different commentators, this work is ascribed both to Vasugupta and to Kallata.

8. No. 511 of the MSS. purchased by Buhler in Kashmir, p. xxxiii, Tour in Search of Sanskrit MSS., etc.

9. The commentator explains the word chaitanya with reference to its formation from chtiti through chētana. A thing can be properly said to exist only when it is cognized by some conscious being. Cognition endows it with Sattva, existential value, as it were; because it manifests what was unmanifested before. Hence cognition is a self-determined activity, not being limited by anything outside itself. In other words chaitanya is characterised by svātantrya, avachchhanda, independence, self-determinedness. This self-determined, cognizing Being is called Spanda in this school.

10. Though all the Āgama schools teach the Advaita, the non-difference, of the individual and supreme souls, they differ from what is popularly called the Advaita school in attributing characteristics, guṇas, in the loose sense of the word, to the supreme soul.

11. Bhēdavādī, one that thinks that each individual Puruṣa is a unit different (bhinna) from the supreme and other Puruṣas. "Separatist" is the nearest English equivalent.

12. In the Shaiva school, all Puruṣas, liberated or not, are called Shivas. Thus there are the Shivas in samsāra, the mukta Shivas, and the anādi Shiva.

13. It is noteworthy that Kṣēmarāja defines the Vedānta, or as he calls it the Vaidika, conception of the ātmā to be identical with the prāṇa. This is quite in keeping with the ideas of the earlier Upaniṣads. Later Vedānta defines the ātmā as sacchidānanda, as is well-known.

14. A datum of consciousness is an ultimate fact that has to be accepted. The Chārvāka argues: "The ātmā is the body, because I am conscious that I am my body." The Shaiva replies: "When I am conscious that I am my body, the consciousness of I is the validating factor whose presence gives a semblance of truth to what the Chārvāka takes to be an ultimate fact. The real datum

of consciousness is the consciousness of I (aham-vimarsha), and not the identification of 'I' with the body, prāṇa, etc.; this ahamvimarsha can be extended to many more objects than the body, *viz.*, prāṇa, buddhi, etc.

15. The "ray of the moon," *i.e.*, consciousness, asserts itself in the very attempt to disprove it. It is an ultimate fact.
16. Sūtras 1 an 2 run as follows: Chaitanyamātmājñānambandhaḥ. This may be (1) chaitanyam ātmā, jñānam bandhaḥ; or, chaitanyam ātmā, ajñānam bandhaḥ. The Sūtra has been so commented on that the meanings of both readings have been woven into one. This has been indicated in the translation by the words ajñāna and jñāna being inserted in appropriate places. This double reading has also been utilised to make the Sūtra refer to the two kinds of āṇava-mala, leading to two forms of bondage explained later.
17. Āṇava-mala, *lit.*, atomic defect, (āṇava, from aṇu, atom), is the consciousness of being a limited being.
18. No. 521 in Buhler's list, p. xxxiv, clxviii Tour, etc.
19. By Abhinava Gupta, the teacher of our commentator.
20. "Kalā to kṣiti," "Kalā, etc." are phrases which frequently occur in Shaiva books meaning "throughout the manifested universe." Kalā, Vidyā, Rāga, Kāla, Niyati, Puruṣa, Pradhāna, Guṇa, and the Sānkhya tattvas from Buddhi to the Earth, are included in the phrase, "Kalā to the earth." For a description of the functions of these tattvas, the reader is referred to my Outlines of Indian Philosophy, pp. 290-292. It is to be noted that the word kalā that immediately succeeds in the Sūtra and is explained in the next paragraph by the commentator has nothing to do with this kalā.
21. According to Hindu philosophy ides are phenomena of matter just as pictures and words are. There is besides an intimate association between ideas and the words that name them. Words are made up of letters, of which also mantras and the names of the goddesses consist.
22. The rope of Brahma, also the rod of Brahma, is the spinal cord, or rather what corresponds to it in the subtle body. It extends

from the Brahma-randhra, the hole of Brahma, anterior fontanelle, to the Chiti. Chiti, lit., pile of wood for burning, is perhaps the Mūlādhāra, the sacral plexus (?) where the fire called Kuṇḍalinī is first kindled by processes of Yoga. Between these two extremities of the rod of Brahma there are several stations here called pīthas, but more usually chakras. Each is presided over by a goddess, a Shakti who has to be mastered to escape being deceived by her. There are other goddesses presiding over other principles also. The power of mantras over these is great. Mātṛikā is the queen of all these and also represents the power of the mantras. Corresponding to the chakras of the body of a man (microcosm) there is the Shakti-Chakra of the universe, driven by the same series of goddesses.

23. "Vāmā and Ichchhā are Brahma and Bhāratī; Jyēṣthā and Jñāna are Hari and Kṣiti; Raudrī Kriyā are Shiva and Aparṇā. Thus is this pair of trinities. The name of the synthesis of each trinity is respectively Shāntā and Ambikā' (Varivasyārahasya, ii. 11-12). Thus the mother of the universe is the synthesis of the three elemental powers, the force of desire, the force of thought, and the force of action (ichchhā-shakti, jñāna-shakti, and kriya-shakti).

24. If there should be an interval without objective cognitions, experienced or remembered, the pure consciousness without the limitation of the objective world will rise; but the Shaktis determine the man so steadily towards the world outside, that it is not possible for such an interval to exist and for the chaitanya to shine in its true light.

25. Pratibhā, knowledge rising without any instrumental cause, *vide* Yog. Sut. ii. 34.

26. In the case of those that steadily practise introspective meditation, there suddenly rises a flash of pure consciousness, during the interval mentioned in the previous Sūtra, when the ātmā shines in its own light. This has to be experienced by each individual for himself. Hence with reference to this experience, each man has to be his own Guru and to enlighten himself, as has been explained by the commentator. Once the experience has been gained, one has to stick to it with udyama (effort). Hence Udyama is Bhairava.

27. "Kālāgni (or Kālānala) to Rasakalā" means the whole of the Brahmāṇda, the Cosmos. The first world (bhuvana) in the Brahmāṇda is where Kālāgni, the fire which destroys the worlds at the beginning of Pralaya, resides. It thus corresponds to the mūlādhāra in the microcosm, where resides the fire which burns up the man's mala, and which is hence the chiti, the funeral pyre of his individuality. The last bhuvana in the Macrocosm is pure Kalā, here called Rasakalā, the ray of pure Ānanda (Tait. Up. ii. 7) also called Shāktātīta Kala, the final stage when liberation is reached. This is the world of Shiva-tattva and corresponds to Brahmarandhra in man.

28. Vyutthāna is "the activity of the mind" (Vyāsa on Yoga-Sūtra III. 38). It is of "three states, kṣipta, mūdha, vikṣipta," (ib. III.9). Kṣipta is the mind "being engaged with objects on account of rajas. Mūdha is being engaged in sleep on account of tamas." Vikṣipta is "being now and then engaged with objects on account of the influence of a little rajas, while being in samādhi on account of excess of sattva. (Vijñāna Bhikṣu on Yoga-Sutra I. 1). Samādhi is the beginning of one-pointedness (Yoga-Sutra III. 11).

29. Thus there are three times three states of mental experience: (1) jāgrat-jāgrat, (2) jāgrat-svapna, (3) jāgrat-suṣupti, (4) svapna-jāgrat, (5) svapna-svapna, (6) svapna-suṣupti, (7) suṣupti-jāgrat, (8) suṣupti-svapna, (9) suṣupti-suṣupti. Of these, the first three are well-known. Kṣēmarāja illustrates the next five in his commentary. Dreams start from a real experience on which the subsequent baseless fabric is woven. This real experience is the jāgrat of svapna. When they end there is a fusion of the cognition and the cognizer, an absence of the distinction of the knower and the known. This is the suṣupti of svapna. The psychological analysis of suṣupti into three stages is, though subtle, not difficult of comprehension. They are the desire to "enter sleep" the beginnings of the obliteration of the sence of the distinction of self and not-self and the utter abolition of cognition during deep sleep when the man is completely enveloped in māyā. It must be remembered that jāgrat, svapna and suṣupti are states of the *Chitta,* mind, and not of the ātmā, which is the changeless, blissful light of consciousness.

30. These four words respectively mean unenlightened, enlightened, developed, well-developed. It is not possible to find out from what "old shāstras" they are taken. The latter three seem to correspond to jāgrat, svapna, and suṣupti of the second of the above interpretation, "according to the Yogis."

31. In the Chhāndogya Upaniṣad, Shrīmantha (the churning of wealth) is described as a rite (V. ii. 4-8) and Shankarāchārya considers it as preliminary to Putramantha (described in Bṛih. Up. VI. iv.)

32. These stages are said to be seven in Yog. Sūt. II. 27.

33. Every novel experience is as it were a challenge to the Ātmā and brings about a flash of its light (*vide* Sūtra V). This occurs also in the course of the mystic experiences of the Yogī, but of course in a greater degree than during the experiences of the ordinary wordly life. When the Yogī has reached the unending bliss of union with his Ātmā he may not be able to retain hold of that state. When he drops down from this exalted state, he again feels wonder. All these are stages of yoga. Kanda, (lit. bulb is the root of the nādis, tubes through which prāṇa, the life-wind circulates. The chief of these nādis is the suṣumṇā, through which travels the fire of kuṇdalinī when roused "Like a gem pierced by a thread the kanda is pierced by suṣumṇa. This chakra in the region of the navel is called maṇipūraka." (Yogachūdāmaṇi Up xii). From the kanda rise fourteen nādis like the spokes of a wheel. It is in the region of the solar plexus. Bindu is the chakra between the eyebrows, called also Bindu-padma, and Ājnā (*vide* Bhāskara Rāya's Lalitāsahasranāma Bhāṣya, nos. 521 & 905). Brahmarandhra is called by some Bindu-mandalam (Ib., No. 380) and is perhaps what is referred to here by the commentator. When the fire of Kuṇdalinī burns in these chakras all limitations are removed and a state higher than the stages above referred to results.

34. The commentary on this Sūtras is rather obscure. Kṛiṣṇadāsa who has versified the Shiva-Sūtra-Vimarshinī into a vārttika, omits the greater part of it.

35. The ordinary unenlightened man (pashu), takes his body to be himself and when his body experiences pain and pleasure, he

says: "I feel pain, I feel pleasure." Not so the Mahāyogī. He knows his real self to be other than his gross body, buddhi, etc. And yet his consciousness pervades the whole universe. Shūnya is the imaginary body in which one feels himself to be in dreams, "Blue etc." means the world of objects.

36. The ordinary man perceives objects by means of his body; during that perception he identifies himself with his body and regards the object as being other than himself. The Yogī's perception extends throughout the world; all the world is his body, and hence to his perception nothing is outside him; yet he does not mistake his body to be his real self.

37. The quotation from Svachchhanda is obscure. It is difficult to guess what are the bhūtas, bhāvas, tattvas and indriyas referred to. Perhaps they mean respectively elements, objects, gross elements, and sense-organs.

38. Amṛita is both immortality in the abstract and the concrete elixir vitae.

39. Krisṇadāsa apparently understands the second differently from how it has been translated above. His vārtika on this passage, literally translated would run thus: "What is bliss of samādhi of him who is a Yogī concentrated on his Self, that in the worlds (macrocosm) is the bliss of the worlds which are being contemplated on within (the mind)." In other words, the bliss of the lokas and the bliss of the self are ultimately the same.

40. Shakti in the macrocosm corresponds to the kuṇḍalini in the human body; Agni and Soma, more usually the sun and the moon, correspond to Idā and Piṅgala, two tenuous tubes (nādis) associated with suṣumṇā.

41. Vibhūtispanda is apparently the part of kārikā where phenomenal powers are described.

42. *vide* ii. 5.

43. *vide* ii. 7.

44. The letters 'A to Ksa' are fifty. The shaktis of the universe from Ichchhā downwards are also fifty. Hence the chain of shaktis corresponds to the alphabet.

45. Prāsāda is a mantra made of the letters 'Ha' and 'Sa.' It, therefore, along with praṇava, refers to the famous mantra, 'om so-ham,' and its reverse 'hamsa,' 'Om soham' leads to union with Shiva and 'Hamsa' with manifested universes.

46. Mantra is derived from "matri, guptabhāṣaṇē." Hence a mantra is that which declares the secret. The text of the vṛitt translated above, refers the idea of 'secret' to the mantra itself. But Kṛiṣṇadāsa defines a mantra in the vārtika of this passage, to be that by which the secret nature of Īshvara is meditated on, thus transferring the adjective to Īshvara's nature.

47. A mantra has already been defined to be a goddess, as a shakti, embodied in a formula. The desire to meditate on it causes a flow of energy in the mind. The attempt not to let it go is the effort that ultimately leads to the union of the devotee and the object of his devotion. It is to be noted that 'bindu' is explained in two ways, (1) mental functioning, (2) supreme light; for every time when the mind strives to fix itself on a mantra, a flash of that supreme light of consciousness illuminates it. Bindu is also the final, fifth part of praṇava, the last echoes of it when pronounced representing the supreme light in the hierarchy of gods. Hence it is said that the pronunciation, *i.e.,* the chanting of praṇava, is the effort that leads the devotee to the Supreme.

48. Consonants are always pronounced joined to 'A,' *e.g.,* 'Ka,' 'Ga,' etc., the relation between consonants and vowels being regarded as similar to that between the body and the life that animates it. Thus as vowels endow consonants with life, so mātṛika endows mantras with life.

49. The passages above-quoted are very obscure. They deal with a subject about which little is known. Even in books intended to be kept concealed, the subject is dealt with in great reserve, because it is both sacred and dangerous.

Parā Shakti is the mother of the universe. She may be conceived as Shiva-shakti, the consciousness of Īshvara. She is Consciousness, Pure, Universal and Unlimited. Hence she is Independence (svachchhaṇda); she is the vibratory energy that drives the cosmos. Being consciousness, she is symbolized by Light; as the light of the sun makes the whole world visible, so she makes cognition, desire and muscular action visible to the man that exercises these functions, *i.e.,* she makes him aware of them. Man in his own real nature is Shiva, but attached to a body and a mind. When these latter act, *i.e.,* when cognition, etc., take place, she turns his attention on them and makes him identify himself with them. She is hence Mahā-Māya, the great deceiver. She is also Mahā-Shakti, the driver of the cosmos; in this she is symbolised by Sound, the greatest manifestation of energy outside us. As Sound symbolizes this aspect of her, individual sounds are the bodies, physical manifestations of parts of her, *viz.,* her attendant divinities, dēvīs, yoginīs, Shaktis, etc. By themselves, these sounds that constitute the mantras, are merely, as it were, dead sound; they become vitalized when one acquires mantravīrya and makes the mantras charged with mystic power (Shakti). This is done by the 'rousing' of Kuṇdalinī. Kuṇdalinī is Parāshakti herself, or rather, a minified replica of her, residing in a man's body. In the case of ordinary men, Kuṇdalinī is potential merely; she resides in the shape of a serpent coiled round his heart. By the word 'heart' is not meant the physiological organ, but the centre of the body imagined as a hollow and filled with ākāsha. Ākāca is sound conceived not as sensation within the brain, but as an ojective entity. Such an ākāsha fills the inside of the body. In its centre, which is the heart, 'the buddhi-guhā,' there is a dot of Light. It is the Shiva, the representative of the supreme in the microcosm. As Shiva's Shakti surrounds Him in the cosmos, so in a man, this dot of Light (bindu) is surrounded by the Shakti in the shape of the sleeping serpent. 'Churning' with the bindu makes the coiled serpent straight. Thus arise Jyēṣthā, Raudrī, Ambā, corresponding respectively from various points of view to Pashyantī, Madhyamā and Vaikharī Vāk, the point, the straight line, and the semi-circle, the one-atomed, the two-atomed, and the three-atomed, etc. By various combinations of these, the mystic correspondence of Shaktis, mantras, sounds, letters, and the states of consciousness referring to these have to be worked out.

50. Bindu and nāda are apparently here used as the names of stages of the growth of the Yogī. Bindu represents the first stage when he has got glimpses of the bindu, the dot of light in the heart, when he first, begins to realise his real nature. Nāda is the first rise of Parāshakti from her sleep and "awakes with a great sound and becomes conscious."

51. Padmāsana is a 'posture' in which the right foot is placed on the left thigh and the left foot on the right thigh, imitating the arrangement of the petals in a lotus. The meditation on the ākāshas and escape from the body riding on the ākāsha is a fairly frequent yogīc practice, though condemned here as not leading to the enlightenment of the man. The three ākāshas mentioned above are those in the three nādis.

52. Krisṇadāsa, quoting from Paratrimshikā, very clearly explains the mātṛikāchakra: The 15 vowels are the 15 tithis. The visarga is the sun and moon. Ka to ma are the 26 tattvas from the earth to puruṣa. Ya to va are Vāyu, Agni, Varuṇa, and Indra. Sha to ha are the 5 Brahmas. He also quotes some other author and makes out ya to va to be the tattvas, māyā to niyati and the 5 letters from cha to be the 5 faces of Shiva, corresponding to the 5 highest tattvas.

53. Perhaps the seven stages of Yoga-Sutras, ii. 27, each sub-divided into a possible sixteen sub-divisions.

54. Puryaṣtaka is the name of the liṅga-dēha in the Shaiva schools. It is eight-fold, being composed of (1) Prakṛiti, (2) Guṇas, (3) Buddhi, (4) Ahaṅkāra, (5) Manas, (6) Organs, (7) Tanmātras, and (8) Bhūtas. Mādhava in chap. vii of Sarvadarshana-saṅgraha discusses this word and tries in a confused manner to reconcile different enumerations of the eight constituents by different writers.

55. This word 'pratyabhijñā occurs casually here; but it has given the Kashmīri Shaiva school its distinctive designation. Utpala called his exposition of the tenets of this school 'Īshvara-Pratyabhijñā-Sūtra,' the Sutras that lead to a recognition of the fact that the individual man is identical with Īshvara; thence the author of Sarva-darshana-saṅgraha called this school 'Pratyabhijñādarshana.' Buhler refers to a Spanda-shāstra different from Pratyabhijñāshāstra. Both shāstras are but one.

56. Kaṅchuka, envelope, is the name of the five tattvas above Puruṣa which envelope man, *viz.*, niyati, kalā, rāga, vidyā, and kāla (*vide* my Outlines of Indian Philosophy, p. 289). Puryaṣtaka, already enumerated, comprises the tattvas below Puruṣa, excluding the sthūladēha. Māyā is the tattva above the pañchakañchuka and is the source of all these.

57. The body is three-fold, sthūla, sūkṣma, para. The last is the one made of the tattvas above māyā, the vidyātattvas and the shivatattva. This body is dissolved on the final attainment of mokṣa.

58. It will be noticed that what is usually understood as yoga in India, is here treated as the lower vidyā, not leading to illumination.

59. The inner prāṇāyāma deals with the inner prāṇa. The outer prāṇa is vāyu, wind. It is the breath in the lungs, the out-breathing being the action of prāṇa, and the in-breathing, of apāna. In the subtle body there is the inner prāṇa, whose upward flow is prāṇa and downward flow is apāna, which take in the nādīs called idā, piṅgalā and suṣumnā. When they are steadied, the fire of udāna rises and they are dissolved.

60. In dhāraṇā, the elements are each confined as it were in their headquarters; the elements are the fundamental sensations, or rather the roots of sensations. It is not possible to find what ghatikā is, unless it is a mistake of some amanuensis for gaṇḍa, the cheek. It is not also possible why the commentator quotes a passage about prāṇāyama to illustrate dhāraṇā.

61. The only entities in the world are Shiva and His Shakti. When this Shakti flows through one of the senses it manifests itself as a sensation. Tanmātra, the root of a sensation, lit., 'that merely,' is pure consciousness showing itself in the limited conditioned form as a sensation. When consciousness manifests itself in the unconditioned form, "the world becomes filled" with its light. When it is withdrawn, the world is emptiness, unreality, non-entity.

62. Evidently the 5 koshas of the Vedāntīs, representing the body.

63. The acting to which the world-process is compared is the primitive "play of shadows" as it is called, which is still played in remote villages. There is only one actor and he sits behind a screen (bhitti) placed on a lighted stage (raṅga) and places on the screen images cut out of leather. The audience sits in the dark place in front of the screen and witnesses the action of the shadows moved by the actor within. The Yogī who has become a muktashiva is hence an actor, the antarātmā, the ātmā within the screen. His karaṇa, instrument, is the antaḥkaraṇa; the

audience, as explained in the next Sūtra is formed by the sense-organs. The light within the screen is the light of consciousness which illuminates the scene and enables the senses to see the performance.

64. The usual reading is 'desiring immortality.' Here 'ashnan' is substituted for 'ichchhan.' I have nowhere else met with this reading.

65. Since the practices condemned in the above quotation are prevalent, the following notes on some of them may be interesting. 'Above' is in the dvādashānta (4th ventricle?); 'below,' in the kanda, region of the navel; 'middle' in the heart; 'before,' etc., the form Sadyojāta and other faces of Shiva; 'ākāsha,' 'making an image of the sun in a part of the ākāsha;' 'below,' in a pit on the ground; 'closing the eyelids,' bringing them together to reduce the sphere of vision; 'binding the eyelids,' fixing them on a tree, a hill, a wall, etc.; 'a support,' giving up one state of consciousness and being fixed in the next; 'the supported' being fixed between two states.

66. Ordinary cognition is bound with the expression thereof in words. Thus the pure cognition and its expression in words are manifestations of the same power. He who cannot exercise jñānashakti without the help of 'sound' *i.e.*, who has not attained to pure consciousness, is a pashu.

67. Following the course of the flame from its origin in the fire, trace how it tapers off till it ends in empty space. So should the manifestation of the ātmā in the body and prāṇa be traced from its grossest manifestations through subtler ones till it dissolves as it were in nothingness. This method of meditation is possible only in a body.

68. The passage quoted is very obscure. But the idea is plain enough. Cognition endows objects with entity, for so long as an object is not cognized it cannot be held to exist—the fundamental idealist position.

INDICES

Index of Words

(The References are to the Unmeṣas and Sūtras)

Abuddha i., 10.
Agni iii., 43.
Agniṣtoma i., 4.
Ahamvimarsha ii., 7.
Ājñā i., 12 *n.*
Ākāsha ii., 3 *n*, 5.
Akhyāti i, 2.
Ambā i., 4, *n* ii, 3.
Āṇava (mala) i, 2, 3, 4.
Āṇava (Upāya) ii., 10; iii. 4, 7, 16, 45
Antarātmā iii., 10.
Aparṇā i., 4 *n.*
Ātmavyāpti iii., 7.
Avīchī i., 7.
Bhairava i., 5, 7, 14; iii. 38.
Bhāratī i. 4 *n.*
Bhūta i., 20.
Bindu ii., 24, 31 *n,* 4 *n.*
Bindu padma, maṇdala i., 12 *n.*
Brahmarandhra i., 4, 12 *n.*
Brahmā, rope of, i., 4 *n.*
Brāhmī (Shakti) i., 4.
Buddha i., 10.
Chaitanyam i., 1.
Chakreshatva i., 20.
Chārvāka i., 1.
Chiti i., 4, *n.*
Chitta ii., 1; iii. 1, 39.
Dhāvaṇa iii., 5, *n.*, 6.

Dhī iii., 12.
Dhyāna iii., 4, 6.
Hamsa ii., 1 *n*.
Hari i., 4 *n*.
Ichchhā (Shakti) i., 4 *n*, 13, 19, 22; ii. 7; iii. 19.
Jāgrat i., 7, 8; ii. 10; iii. 8, 9.
Jīva iii., 4.
Jñāna (Shakti) i., 4, *n*, 13, 19; ii. 7; iii. 19, 29.
Jyeṣthā i., 4; ii. 3, *n*.
Kalā(=function) i., 3.
Kālāgni i., 6, *n*; iii. 4.
Kālānala i., 6.
Kañchuka ii., 3 *n*.
Kanda i., 12 *n*.
Kāraṇa shakti iii., 36.
Karma (mala) i., 3, 4.
Karmātmā iii., 35.
Kēvalī iii. 34.
Khēcharī i., 22; ii. 5, 7.
Kriyā (Shakti) i., 4 *n*, 3, 19; iii. 19, 30, 81.
Kṣiti i., 3 *n*, 4 *n*.
Kumārī i., 13.
Kuṇdalinī i., 12 *n*; ii. 3, *n*, 4.
Laukika i., 1.
Madhyamā ii., 3 *n*.
Mādhyamika i., 1.
Mahāhrada i., 22; ii. 3.
Mahā Māyā ii., 3 *n*, 4.
Mala i., 2, 3, 4.
Mantra ii, 1.
Mantravīrya i., 22; ii. 3.
Matṛikā mālinī i., 22; ii. 3.
Mātṛikā i., 4; ii. 3.
Mātṛikā chakra ii., 7.
Māyā i., 3, 10.
Māyā (mala) i., 3, 4.
Māyā (tattva) iii., 6.
Mitasiddhi iii., 6.
Nāda ii. 4 *n*.
Nādī i., 12 n; iii. 3.

Nāgabodhi Int, i, *n*.
Padmāsana ii., 5 *n*.
Parā Bhattāraka i., 22.
Parāhantā i., 22.
Parāshakti i., 13; ii. 3, *n*; iii. 15, 19.
Pashu i., 15.
Pashushakti i., 16.
Pashyantī ii., 3, *n*.
Pītha i., 4.
Prabuddha i., 10.
Prāṇa i., 12 *n*.
Prāṇāyāma iii., 5 *n*, 6.
Prasāda ii., 1 *n*.
Pratibhā i., 5.
Pratyabhijñā iii., 2.
Pratyāhāra iii., 5, 6.
Puryaṣtaka iii., 21 *n*, 3, 10.
Rasakalā i., 5 *n*.
Raudrī i., 4; ii. 3, *n*.
Rodhinī ii., 3.
Sadāshiva i., 14, 16.
Sahajavidyā iii., 17, 18.
Samādhi i., 7, 10, 18; iii. 5, 44.
Sattvasiddhi iii., 12.
Shākta (Stage) i., 5; iii. 16.
Shākta (upāya) ii., 1, 10, iii. 7.
Shaktichakra i., 4, 5, 11, 21.
Shāmbhava (stage) i, 5; iii. 16.
Shāmbhava (upāya) i., 22.
Shānta i., 4 *n;* iii, 4.
Shivas i., 1 *n*.
Shivavyāpti ili., 7.
Shrīmanthānubhairava i., 10.
Shuddha tattva i., 16.
Shuddha vidyā i., 20; ii, 10; iii. 16.
Shūnya i., 1. 15; iii. 10.
Soma i, 19; iii. 43.
Spanda *Int.* i., *n*; ii. 10; iii. 6.
Sthūladēha iii., 3.
Suprabuddha i., 10.

Suprashānta iii., 6.
Sūrya i., 19; iii. 43.
Suṣupti i., 7, 10.
Svapva i., 7, 9; ii. 10.
Tanmātra iii 9 *n*.
Tattvas, enumerated i, 3, *n*.
Turya i, 7, 10; iii. 20, 23, 32.
Turyātīta i, 10; iii. 23.
Udāna iii. 6.
Udyama i., 5.
Umā i., 12.
Unmanā iii., 7, 45.
Unmēṣa i., 5.
Vaikharī ii., 3 *n*.
Vāmā i., 4.
Vāsanā i., 4.
Vasugupta *Int*, i.
Vedānti i., 1.
Vibhūti Spanda i., 20, *n*.
Vidyā ii. 3.
Vimarsha iii., 44.
Vināyakas ii., 10; iii, 23.
Vīresha i., 11.
Vitarka i., 17.
Vyutthāna i., 5, 17; iii. 23.
Yogabhūmika i., 12.
Yogāchāra i., 1.
Yogamāyā i. 13.
Yoginī *Int*. i., *n*.
Yoni i., 3; iii. 19.

II. Index of Anonymous Early Āgama Works Quoted

Ānandabhaīrava, iii. 22.
Bhargashikhā, i., 6.
Chandrajñāna i., 7. 18.
Jñānagarbha iii., 21.
Kālikākrama iii. 25, 26, 31, 34, 35, 40, 44.
Kulachūḍāmaṇi ii., 5.

Kulapañchāshikā iii., 24.
Kularatnamāha iii., 42.
Kulasāra i. 12.
Lakṣmikaulārṇava i., 16, 19; iii. 7.
Mālinīvijaya 1, 2, 3, 5, 6, 22; ii. 6, 9; iii. 19, 23, 24.
Mantrasadbhāva ii., 1, 3, 3; iii. 2, 3.
Mṛityujidbhattāraka i., 1, 13, 19; iii. 15, 16, 13, 21, 80, 42.
Sarvāchāra i., 2.
Sarvamaṅgalā iii, 8.
Sarvavira i., 4.
Srikanthesha Samhitā ii. 1; iii. 18.
Shrī Pūrva ii. 10.
Sūkṣmabhairava i., 6.
Siddhāmṛita ii., 7.
Svachchhanda i., 3, 5, 11, 13, 15, 24; iii. 5, 7, 10, 18, 14, 17, 18, 21, 24, 26, 36, 40, 43, 45.
Tantrasadbhāva ii., 5.
Tttvagarbha iii., 37.
Timirodghāta i., 4; ii, 8; iii, 19.
Trikahṛidaya i. 1.
Vijñānabhairava i., 1, 14, 15, 16, 17; ii, 8, 9; iii. 2, 4, 8, 21, 27, 38, 39, 44.
Vijñānabhattāraka i., 18.
Vijñana uttara ii. 1.
Vīrāvali i. 6.

III. Index of Later Shaiva Works or Authors Quoted or Referred to

Abhinavagupta's *Pārātrimshikavivaraṇa* and *Tantrāloka* ii. 7.
Abhinavagupta's *Īshvarapratyabhijnā-Sūtra-Vimarṣhini* iii. 33.
Kallata's *Vṛitti (Spandasarvasva?)* ii., 8.
Kallata's *Tattvārthachūdāmaṇi* (said to be the fourth Kāṇda of his Vṛitti, iii., 43.
Kṣēmarāja's *Svachchhandodyota* i. 2. -Do- *Spandanirṇaya Int.* i., 19.
(Bhatta) Nārāyaṇa iii., 9.
(Shrī) Nātha iii., 13.
Utpala Deva ii., 7.
-Do- *Īshvarapratyabhijñā Sūtrā* i., 2, 3; iii. 9, 17, 22, 37.

IV. Index of Other Works Quoted or Referred to

Bhagavad Gita (iv. 27.) ii. 8.
Katha Upaniṣad (iv. i.) iii. ii.
Naishvāsadēvīmaheshvara Nātaka (vii.) iii. 9.
Pāṇini's *Dhātupātha* i., 13.
Patañjali's *Sūtra* (iii. 38.) ii. 4.

Unidentified

Agama ii. 7; iii. 4, 28.
Vājasaneya iii. 48.

V. Index of References to Spanda Kārikā

[*Note.*: The *Spanda Kārikā,* being professedly a re-statement of the teaching of the Shiva-Sūtra, except the Āṇavopayā, Kṣemarājā, in his commentaries, points out the passages of the *Spanda Kārikā,* corresponding to each Sūtra.]

	Shiva-Sūtra	Spanda Karikā.
i.	1. ...	6, 7, 2, 5, 28, 29.
	2. ...	9, 4, 6.
	3. ...	9.
	4. ...	45, 47.
	5. ...	4.
	6. ...	1, 52.
	7. ...	3.
	11. ...	17.
	12. ...	11.
	13. ...	8.
	14. ...	29.
	15. ...	39.
	16. ...	30.
	17. ...	32.
	18. ...	32.
	19. ...	33, 34.
	20. ...	38, 36, 37, 40.
	21. ...	43.
	22. ...	26.

ii.	1. ...	27.
	2. ...	31.
	3. ...	26, 27.
	4. ...	42.
	5. ...	9.
	6. ...	62.
	8. ...	9.
	9. ...	44.
	10. ...	35, 21.
iii.	2. ...	49, 50.
	3. ...	20.
	14. ...	7.
	17. ...	30.
	32. ...	14, 15, 10.

VI. Index of Works Quoted In the Foot-Notes

Bhāskara Rāya's *Lalitāsahasranāma Bhāṣya* (Nos. 380, 521, 905) i. 12.
Brihadāraṇyaka Upaniṣad (iv. 4) i. 11.
Chhāndogya Upaniṣad (v. 2) i. 11.
Kṛiṣṇadāsa's Vārtika on Shiva-Sūtra i. 12, 18; ii. 1, 7.
Outlines of Indian Philosophy (by the Translator) (pp. 290-292) i. 3.
(pp. 289) iii. 3.
Sarvadarshanasaṅgraha (vii.) iii. 2.
Shāṅkara Bhāṣya (on *Chh-up.* v. 2) i. 11.
Taittiriya Upaniṣad (ii. 7.) i. 6.
Varivasyārahasya (ii. 11-12) i. 4.
Vijñāna Bhikṣu on *Yog. Sūt.* (i. 1.) i. 7.
Vyāsa on *Yog. Sūt.* (iii. 38) i. 7.
Yogachūdāmaṇi Upaniṣad (xii) i. 2.
Yoga Sūtras (ii. 27) i. 12.
(ii. 34) i. 5.
(iii. 9-11) i. 7.